Start Your Own

HAIR SALON AND DAY SPA

Additional titles in *Entrepreneur's* **Startup Series**

Start Your Own

Bar and Tavern

Bed & Breakfast

Business on eBay

Business Support Service

Car Wash

Child Care Service

Cleaning Service

Clothing Store

Coin-Operated Laundry

Consulting

Crafts Business

e-Learning Business

Event Planning Business

Executive Recruiting Service

Freight Brokerage Business

Gift Basket Service

Growing and Selling Herbs and Herbal
  Products

Home Inspection Service

Import/Export Business

Information Consultant Business

Lawn Care Business

Mail Order Business

Medical Claims Billing Service

Personal Concierge Service

Personal Training Business

Pet-Sitting Business

Restaurant and Five Other Food Businesses

Self-Publishing Business

Seminar Production Business

Specialty Travel & Tour Business

Staffing Service

Successful Retail Business

Vending Business

Wedding Consultant Business

Wholesale Distribution Business

Entrepreneur
MAGAZINE'S

start*up*

2ND EDITION

Start Your Own

HAIR SALON AND DAY SPA

Your Step-by-Step Guide to Success

Entrepreneur Press and Eileen Figure Sandlin

EP
Entrepreneur.
Press

Jere L. Calmes, Publisher
Managing Editor: Marla Markman
Cover Design: Beth Hansen-Winter
Production and Composition: Eliot House Productions

This publication is designed to provide accurate and authoritative information in regard to the subject matter covered. It is sold with the understanding that the publisher is not engaged in rendering legal, accounting or other professional services. If legal advice or other expert assistance is required, the services of a competent professional person should be sought.

Library of Congress Cataloging-in-Publication Data
Sandlin, Eileen Figure.
  Start your own hair salon/by Eileen Sandlin.—2nd ed.
  p. cm.
  Prev. published under title: Start your own hair salon and day spa.
  Includes index.
  ISBN–13: 978-1-59918-346-6 (alk. paper)
  ISBN–10: 1-59918-346-3
  1. Beauty shops—United States—Management. 2. Health resorts—United States—Management. I. Title.
  TT965.S26 2010
  646.7'2068—dc22   2010004883

Printed in Canada

14 13 12 11 10   10 9 8 7 6 5 4 3 2 1

Contents

▲

Preface

Are you looking for a business that's personally rewarding, makes a lot of people happy, can be very lucrative, and is recession-proof? If you'll settle for three out of four (since no business can completely escape the impact of a down economy), then you've come to the right place.

The book you're holding will give you all the practical advice you need to build the foundation for and launch a full-service hair salon and day spa. That includes information you'll need to handle the myriad details that go into starting and operating a small business, from analyzing your market, writing a business plan and establishing an internet presence to finding financing and handling all the other day-to-day duties necessary to keep your business running like a well-oiled machine. It's possible to do these things well whether you're a practicing cosmetologist who's decided the time is right to strike out on your own, or a business manager who can see the potential in this always-dynamic, always-growing industry. All it takes is determination, hard work, optimism, and a willingness to learn anything related to business management that you don't already know.

Of course, it does help to have a strong business background and a good head for numbers, even if the extent of your experience is accurately calculating the government's lamentable bite out of your tip income, balancing your checkbook, or managing a household budget. Previous college coursework in disciplines like accounting and business management is even better. But as the saying goes, where there's a will, there's a way, and if you're determined to be successful, your chances of achieving your dreams increase significantly.

Toward that end, this how-to volume contains many resources that will help you find your own little piece of "shear" heaven. There are step-by-step instructions for important tasks like selecting the appropriate legal structure for your salon and coordinating an advertising program. There are worksheets that can help you calculate costs, keep expenditures under control, and stay organized. There are also names and addresses (both snail and cyber) of numerous industry organizations and government agencies that can provide valuable information.

But perhaps most important, there are tips and advice from industry insiders, including numerous salon owners and other stars of the beauty industry universe who lent their voices and vision to this project by agreeing to be interviewed, sometimes for hours at a time and sometimes in the wee morning hours before their businesses opened or well into the night. No doubt they were so generous with their time because they know the value of leading by example, and you'll hear from them often in the pages of this book because firsthand experience truly is a great teacher. What's more, they've all agreed to be personal resources for you in case you have questions that only another experienced salon/spa owner/manager can answer. You'll find contact information for these gracious folks in the Appendix.

By the way, what you won't find in these pages is instructions for giving a great razor cut, rolling perms, or foiling hair. Frankly, that instruction is best left to the pros at cosmetology schools and other beauty industry sources. And since there's a good chance you're already practicing the craft of beauty as a profession, you probably don't need help in that area anyway. Or if you're a business/marketing type, you'll probably never have the slightest inclination to start shearing heads.

So turn the page and let's start rolling!

Hair Today, Hair Tomorrow

Housing values may plummet. Retirement funds may shrink. Hurricanes may howl maniacally and exotic viruses may spread unchecked. But despite manmade and natural disasters, hair still grows, and people still need pampering. So no matter what the state of the economy and the world we live in, it's still a good time to start a hair salon and day spa, and the prospects for "shear" success are excellent.

According to a *Modern Salon* survey, there were 400,000 hair salons in the United States in a recent year. The salon service industry had revenues of $60 billion, which included $23 billion generated by hair cut services and $5.5 billion by retail hair care product sales. In addition, the National Accrediting Commission of Cosmetology Arts and Services reports that the demand for trained cosmetologists has continued to grow over the past 10 years.

How is it possible for a service sector like the beauty industry to continue to thrive given the fluctuations of the economy? No doubt because many of the services offered by salons simply can't be duplicated at home—or at least not duplicated well. In addition, in an age where people freely shell out $5 for a cup of coffee, the price of a haircut probably doesn't seem very high considering the lift it can give your spirits. Also, the baby boomers, who now constitute the largest population segment in America, are more than willing and are still financially able to spend money on any personal care service they perceive will make them look younger and more attractive. No doubt as a result of their driving desire for a youthful appearance, the hair color segment of the salon industry continues to grow, according to Professional Consultants and Resources, a Plano, Texas, marketing and consulting firm. Coloring alone brought in $10.4 billion for the beauty industry in a recent year.

The spa industry also is faring well. According to the International Spa Association, the U.S. spa industry had revenues of $10.9 billion in 2008, generated by 138 million spa visits. It's estimated there are 32.2 million active spa-goers, 34 percent of whom are men.

Earning Potential

What all this prosperity means to you is that the prospects for people who own personal care businesses are bright. The most recent Job Demand Survey, distributed by the National Accrediting Commission of Cosmetology Arts and Sciences, indicated that average total income (including tips) for salon owners was $53,150, although it's possible to earn much more depending on where and how you do business. For instance, two salon owners interviewed for this book earned $120,000 in a recent year.

A search of the internet revealed that there's no other data to indicate exactly how well the owners of salon/spas are doing. Suffice it to say that total wages and salaries for the estimated 303,700 employees in the spa industry were almost $5 billion across the entire industry in the past few years.

A Look Back

Although the recent interest in personal care services may seem like a new trend, the reality is that hair care has long been a part of human culture . . . in fact, probably for as long as humans have been on the planet. The earliest record of personal hair care dates back 2.5 million years ago, when brushes used to create cave paintings in Spain and France were adapted for use in hair grooming. More recently, archeologists have found evidence that cosmetics were used by the Egyptians as early as the fourth millennium B.C. (for proof, just check out the golden sarcophagus of the boy king Tutankhamen with its heavily painted visage), as well as ancient artifacts of eye makeup.

Although hairdressing techniques have evolved throughout the ages, some things have stayed the same. Primitive men, including Native Americans, tied feathers, beads, and other objects into their hair, which they wore long and flowing to denote status and intimidate enemies. Persian noblemen curled their hair and beards, and even used henna to stain them red. Men often wore wigs throughout the ages, including during the 18th century when their wigs were powdered and styled with queues, or long ponytails, that hung down their backs. Women were equally fashionable throughout history, using yellow soap to dye their hair blonde in republican Rome, or coiling their tresses into styles that at times were covered by cauls (nets) or embellished with jewels or golden ornaments.

Fun Fact
The first known school for hairdressing in the United States was established in Chicago in 1890.

Interestingly, many of the innovations in hair design that are still with us today originated in the late 19th century. The Marcel wave, also known as the finger wave, was first created around 1890 using heated irons. The hot-blast dryer, which evolved into today's blow dryer, was also invented at that time. Madam C.J. Walker, a former slave, formulated products that could soften and straighten the hair of black women. She later became the first African American woman to earn $1 million. The first electric haircutter, consisting of a comb with a platinum wire that was heated and used to burn off the ends of the hair, was invented around the turn of the century.

A Look Forward

It wasn't uncommon for hair to be scorched by hot tools until it was the texture of coarse wool. Nowadays, hair-care techniques are much gentler, and the reasons people choose to visit salons are diverse. They include:

- Wanting to look great for a special occasion, like the prom, a wedding, or a party.
- Wanting the same 'doo as a favorite celebrity (who could forget Jennifer Aniston's choppy layers or Farrah Fawcett's feathered sides?).
- Wanting to change a look by perming, coloring, or straightening tresses.
- Wanting to correct the damage caused by overprocessing done by amateurs.
- Wanting to update a look (like eschewing the Jackie Kennedy bob worn since she was the First Lady).
- Wanting to look like a new person (like going from mousy brown to ravishing red).

All this is good news, considering the bad hairdos that have been popular in recent decades (think mullets and technicolor mohawks) and the trend toward gleaming chrome domes as sported by NBA players in the past decade. So now your mission, should you choose to accept it, is to start a great new salon with the right rep so people will leave the boring salon they've been frequenting and make a mad dash to your door.

The Opportunities

There are three ways you can make your mark on the hair industry. You can open a franchise hair salon, in which you pay money upfront for the privilege of opening that salon using someone else's established name (which gives you an instant reputation) and its resources (like advertising campaigns). You can buy an established salon from someone who's retiring from the business, has tired of the business, or has damaged the business and forced it into bankruptcy (all three happen every day). You can establish your own salon using your own money, your own ingenuity and your own optimism that hard work and talent will win out.

While you'll find a list of well-known hair franchises in the Appendix of this book, the real focus of this how-to guide will be on starting your own salon/spa from scratch. And just as a side note: While the term "salon" is used throughout the book, it's meant to include both salon and day spa services, as the title on the cover of the book indicates. Since the tools necessary to open both are basically the same, it seemed redundant to say "salon/spa" over and over. The specifics relating to the spa end of the business, from

Stat Fact
There are approximately 1.6 million cosmetology professionals employed in salons and barber shops in the United States

the types of equipment needed to the types of services offered, are discussed in detail in Chapter 8.

By the way, before we move on to the nuts and bolts—or shall we say the shampoo and conditioner—of the salon industry, there's one more type of salon that bears mentioning here because it's so prevalent in the beauty business. Booth rental salons are owned by a person (or persons) who's basically the landlord for a group of hairstylists and other service providers working under his or her roof. As the landlord, the salon owner/operator collects a flat monthly fee from the service providers, for which they have the privilege of using salon space and nonremovable equipment like a styling station and chair. The renters, in turn, are considered independent contractors who must provide their own supplies (everything from hair dryers to perm rods), set their own hours, book their own appointments, and have their own key to the building.

Or at least that's the way the IRS expects booth rentals to work. If you pay your renters a commission, provide items like back-bar supplies and towels, schedule appointments, process credit card transactions, and/or offer benefits like paid vacations and insurance, then you have employees rather than independent contractors. And you can be sure that the IRS won't smile benevolently on your fledgling business venture if you try to pass your renters off as independent contractors.

If you'd like to know more about the distinctions between employees and independent contractors like booth renters, download a copy of Publication 1779, *Independent Contractor or Employee*, from the IRS website at irs.gov. But for the purposes of this book, it's assumed that you're not establishing a booth rental operation, but rather a full-fledged salon and day spa.

So what does it take to be a successful salon/spa entrepreneur? First, it helps to be a risk taker, says John Palmieri, owner of Scizzors in Shrewsbury, Massachusetts. "It's to your advantage to jump in and just do it," Palmieri says. "Don't overanalyze the process or you won't get anything done. Take a chance—open the door and start letting customers in."

Leslie Rice, co-owner of Goldwaves Salon and Spa in Fort Worth, Texas, believes you have to be willing to try anything to succeed. "If you're scared, you'll hinder your growth. Instead, go for it, then re-evaluate what doesn't work and fix it," Rice says.

"You have to be able to see the big picture and not get bogged down in the details," says Sasha Rash, owner of La Jolie Salon in Princeton, New Jersey.

According to Vander E. Harris Jr., former president of the National Black Hair Association, "You have to have determination and an entrepreneurial mindset to be successful. You also need vision and goals."

A thirst for knowledge, a strong constitution, and an indefatigable spirit are also traits the entrepreneurs interviewed for this book said were necessary for success. Now add a dash of humor and a pinch of determination to the mixture, and you definitely have a recipe for success. We'll help you get rolling with advice from this book. In the meantime, think you're cut out to own and run a salon? Take the Salon Savvy Survey below to find out.

Salon Savvy Survey

Take this short quiz to see if you have what it takes to be a successful salon/spa owner:

1. Can you supervise and motivate giggly teens, chatty 20-somethings, menopausal manicurists, and the other 64 common types of employees?
❑ Yes   ❑ No

2. Has your hair been at least two different colors in the past six months?
❑ Yes   ❑ No

3. Can you juggle up to a dozen tasks at once for 12 hours straight and still have enough energy to drive home at night?   ❑ Yes   ❑ No

4. Do you prefer to nap in the nearest hydraulic chair rather than go home?
❑ Yes   ❑ No

5. Do you do windows and fold towels?   ❑ Yes   ❑ No

6. Do you like to do windows and fold towels?   ❑ Yes   ❑ No

7. Can you write massive tax payment checks to the IRS every quarter without staging a four-county taxpayer revolt?   ❑ Yes   ❑ No

8. Would red ink on your balance statement make you sob more than the film *An Affair to Remember*?   ❑ Yes   ❑ No

9. Would you cringe if someone playfully referred to your salon as a "clip joint"?
❑ Yes   ❑ No

10. Do you automatically rotate hair-care product bottles on the shelf so the labels are facing out, even in the grocery store?   ❑ Yes   ❑ No

Scoring

9–10 yes: You're a shear genius.

5–8 yes: Your career is lookin' good.

1–4 yes: Better get set for a long learning curl.

0 yes: Keep buying those lottery tickets.

The Salon Scene

Before we delve into the myriad details that go into establishing a salon and day spa, let's take a look at the numerous services typically offered by today's *maison de beauté* (or house of beauty, if you avoided French 101 in high school). Naturally, there are more services described in this chapter than you could possibly hope to offer when you first go

▲

into business. So in Chapter 3, we'll discuss how you can analyze your market area to determine which of these services might be the most attractive to your target audience and make the most money for you. But in the meantime, we've presented every possible option here so it will be easier for you to make some choices later, when you formulate your business plan.

Also included in this chapter is a brief overview of the day-to-day operations involved in keeping a salon and spa humming along, as well as a discussion of the decisions you must make early on to put your salon development project into motion.

Chop Shop

On the hair salon side, the most sought-after service is, of course, haircutting and styling. This includes everything from styles created with a blow dryer, curling iron, or hand scrunching to tried-and-true roller/dryer sets for senior citizens. Popular color services include highlighting, low lighting, glazing, corrective coloring, dimensional special effects, and hair and scalp treatments. Texture services include permanent waves, partial or spot perms, spiral perms, and anti-curl treatments. Braiding falls into a category of its own. There actually are many salons that specialize in nothing but this particular hair art, but there's no reason you can't offer it in your salon, too. Just keep in mind that it's a very time-consuming service and many of the most successful braiding salons have two or more stylists working on one client at the same time. Finally, special-occasion hairstyling, for events like proms and weddings, rounds out the typical hair services menu.

Although technically an aesthetic service, nail and foot care are often offered in hair salons. Nail services include:

- Acrylic nail application
- Manicures (both traditional and French)
- Nail tipping
- Nail wrapping
- Paraffin treatments
- Pedicures
- Sculpted nail application
- Skin exfoliation and hand/foot massage are often part of the manicure and pedicure processes.

Selecting Services

As mentioned in the previous chapter, this book was developed on the premise that you will be establishing a full-service salon rather than a family hair salon that concentrates on quick-turnover services like haircuts and perms. As a result, you should plan to offer the full range of hair care services mentioned earlier. Of course, the number of special services you provide may be limited by the proficiency of the help you hire and the training you can offer them, but at the very least, you should offer haircuts and styling, basic perms, straightening treatments, and color services.

Whether you offer nail services or not is entirely dependent on the size of your salon and whether you can afford both the equipment and the salary of a nail technician at the outset. Today's nail client is used to visiting shops devoted only to nail services, so she

---

It's a Man's World

It wasn't so long ago that no self-respecting male would be caught dead in a day spa. But all that has changed with the aging of the baby boomers, who are devoted to looking youthful, staying healthy, and being fit.

The International Spa Association reported recently that 34 percent of spa clients are men, who are usually introduced to the spa experience by their wives or girlfriends. (Hold the pink robes, please.) Their number-one choice of service is massage. So as you plan your day spa, be sure to include amenities for men.

Design the spa with separate waiting and changing areas for men, and stock them with men's magazines, and maybe even a TV tuned to ESPN. Stock up on spa products with a more masculine scent (something woodsy or musky). Then attract men to your facility by running special promotions just for them, such as "Stress Relief Night for Men." You might even offer bachelor party packages.

Or you could try offering men-only spa services like Ben Davis does in The Gent's Place, his combination barbershop, spa, and men's club, which he opened in Frisco, Texas, in 2008. "I built The Gent's Place with the neighborhood barbershop of the past in mind but with all the amenities and services that the modern gentleman requires to keep a consistent and professional look," says Davis.

In addition to spa and barbershop services—haircuts, color, massage, shaves, facials, and "hand and foot repairs" (rather than "manis" and "pedis")—The Gent's Place offers a bar waiting area equipped with HDTV and a selection of complimentary beer, whisky, and wine. "If you're getting lousy haircuts and poor service from the discount chains or being 'womanized' at your wife's salon, it's time to man up," says Davis.

The Gent's Place isn't the only place to "man up" in the United States. Dallas has several men-only spas, one of which services up to 130 clients on Saturdays alone. It's definitely a trend that bears watching.

won't be surprised if you don't offer manicures, acrylic nails, and tipping. But you may be able to get her to leave her regular manicurist if she sees that you're offering the same service at your cool new salon. We'll talk about equipment in Chapter 7 and salaries in Chapter 9, so you can table your decision about whether to include nail services for now.

Smoothing and Soothing

As mentioned in the last chapter, spa services continue to be a strong segment of the personal care industry. The range of services is truly dazzling, but basically, aesthetic services offered at a day spa fall into three categories: skin and body care, hair removal, and makeup. Technically, there's a fourth category—nail services—but as we just mentioned, nail services have crossed over into the beauty mainstream and are no longer considered just a spa service. However, when offered in a spa setting, nail services tend to be higher priced than in a salon.

Skin- and body-care spa services include:

- Facials and body exfoliation (which may involve the use of salt glows, body polish, enzyme peels, and body masks like mud or paraffin)
- Massage (full body massage, facial and/or hand/foot massage)
- Wraps and packs (used to combat cellulite and reduce water retention)
- Hydrotherapy treatments (whirlpool baths, Scotch hose—a type of massage that uses a hose to direct streams of water on the body to improve circulation— and hot tub treatments)
- Body tanning (self-tanners and tanning beds)

Hair-removal services include:

- Electrolysis
- Eyebrow arching
- Waxing (face, legs, arms, bikini, back, and underarms)

Makeup services include:

- Color analysis
- Cosmetics application
- Ear piercing
- Eyebrow tinting
- Eyelash tinting

These services and the equipment necessary to offer them are discussed in detail in Chapter 8.

When determining which of these spa services to offer, it's important to weigh factors like equipment cost against potential profitability. For instance, you may be a great believer in the benefits of hydrotherapy and would like to offer it in your new day spa, but hydrotherapy services require the greatest outlay of cash for equipment and facility development. So unless you have sufficient startup capital (and a significant amount of space to boot), it might be a better idea to limit your spa services initially to massage (which doesn't require as much equipment or space) and/or facials. Then, when you're operating profitably, you can expand your facility or move to a new one that will allow you to increase the scope of your day spa services.

> ### Smart Tip
>
> **Tip...**
>
> Products perceived to have anti-aging properties, like "natural" cosmetics and spa products with ingredients like green tea, grapeseed extract, and clay and sea minerals, continue to be popular among American consumers, says Euromonitor International, a provider of global consumer business intelligence. So you should add them to your salon and spa product lineup as a way to increase sales.

Another important factor to consider when deciding which spa services you'll offer is that many of them require a wet room. This includes the hydrotherapies mentioned above, as well as any body masks, exfoliation treatments, and other body treatments that must be rinsed off after application. Even if you decide not to offer hydro services when you first open, you should at least plan to include a wet room in your initial plans or you'll always be limited to "dry" services—unless, of course, you move to new digs or expand your existing location.

There's yet another compelling reason for offering wet services. "Water treatments are the very nature of a spa," says Colleen Blevins-Lunsford, the former owner of Wolf Mountain Day Spa in Grass Valley, California, who recently met the man of her dreams and moved to England. "Spas are about health and wellness, and for centuries man and beast alike have found healing and cures from the ocean, moor bogs, natural springs, and so on. If [water] treatments are not offered, then the spa is considered a skin-care salon or clinic."

Because the concept of a day spa implies a day of pampering similar to what you might enjoy on a spa vacation or a cruise ship, it's common for spa owners to offer packages of services. Generally speaking, packages should consist of at least three complementary services, or in the case of hydrotherapy treatments, one hydro service and up to four "dry" services. Spa industry insiders recommend offering half-day packages that run about three hours and full-day, five-hour packages that include 30 minutes to an hour for a light lunch.

Sample packages might include:

- Manicure, pedicure, makeup, hair styling (half day)
- Salt glow rub, body sugaring, full body massage (half day)
- Hot stone therapy, stone manicure and pedicure (half day)
- Scotch hose hydrotherapy, full-body mask, Swedish massage (full day)
- Hydrotherapy tub, mud body wrap, full-body massage, herbal facial (full day)
- Sea salt exfoliation, Vichy shower, massage, spa lunch (full day)
- Anti-aging facial treatment, deep-tissue massage, scalp treatment, facial (full day)

Stat Fact
In 1987, there were 30 day spas in the United States, according to The Spa Expert at the Marshall Plan, a Venice, California–based communications firm specializing in spas and resorts. By 2008, the number of day spas had risen to nearly 14,500, and spa visits increased 25 percent from 2007 to 2008, according to the International Spa Association.

Spa packages often have colorful and evocative names that bring to mind relaxing vacation retreats. Examples include Tropical Indulgence (for a seaweed wrap and coconut facial) and Calming Waters Escape (for a variety of relaxing hydro services).

Beauty Business Basics

Before we start delving into the intricacies of the services you can expect to offer as a new hair salon/day spa owner, let's take a global look at the business, from day-to-day operations to price-setting.

A Day in the Life

Even though no two days tend to be alike for salon owners because the needs of their clients (not to mention their employees) vary so widely, there are certain tasks you can expect to perform on a regular basis. To begin with, you'll probably spend a lot of time on the telephone every day, helping to book appointments, ordering supplies, talking to salespeople, arranging for in-shop or offsite training, and so on. You'll also have to make up work schedules (then juggle them to accommodate employees' scheduled time off and personal needs), track receivables, monitor costs, dream up new advertising and marketing strategies, and possibly create daily or weekly specials that can be e-mailed or "tweeted" to your regular customers to lure them in for additional services. On the personnel side, you'll hire new employees, visit beauty schools to troll for hot prospects, conduct performance reviews, mentor young stylists and/or aesthetics technicians with minimal experience, consult with stylists or colorists whose efforts go awry, squelch gossip, and mediate when tempers flare between staff members. And of course, if you're also a licensed practicing cosmetologist, you'll be styling hair, applying color, and rolling perms.

Sounds like a lot for one person to do, doesn't it? Well, it is—and that's why many salon owners (even those whose salons are small) hire a salon manager to take over some of the administrative duties. This is a particularly good idea if you intend to continue to work behind the chair, since hairstyling chores alone can take up a lot of your time every day. And while it's possible to slip in some administrative work while you're waiting for someone's perm to process or a late client to arrive, it can be difficult to switch gears and give administrative tasks, like balancing the books, the full concentration they need.

You'll find a detailed discussion about hiring and managing administrative and salon/spa employees in Chapter 9.

By now it should be obvious that attention to detail is one of the most important personal traits a salon owner must have. You can make it easier to keep track of all the details related to running your salon by investing in a good planner to help you keep appointments and activities straight and on schedule. A Franklin planner, DayTimer, or other notebook-style planner will work just fine if you prefer to work on paper. But if you're a techie, you might like to use a mobile pocket PC, smartphone, software program, or online tool instead.

Known until recently as PDAs (for "personal digital assistant") pocket PCs don't have built-in voice communication capability but do offer many other useful features like a digital camera, texting capability, and oh yes—a calendar function. A couple to check out include the Dell Axim and the HP iPAC.

If you use a cell phone a lot, you'll probably prefer a mobile Smartphone instead since it combines the functions of a PDA with voice communication tools. The iPhone and BlackBerry are fully featured smartphones that are worth a look.

Stat Fact

There are 825,000 people employed in personal appearance jobs (like barbering and cosmetology), according to the latest edition of the BLS's *Occupational Outlook Handbook*.

You also can use calendar software or online calendars, such as the Google Calendar, to keep track of your appointments. Just Google "calendar software" for a selection of choices. In addition, Microsoft Word has 30 built-in calendar templates, which you can print out for easy access, or save to your computer so you can make electronic notations. To find the templates, open a new document and search for "calendar."

Finally, the hair salon software packages discussed in Chapter 7 include calendars, so if you're planning to use salon software, you might want to hold off on buying standalone calendar software until you see what the salon software can do.

In the meantime, if you want additional information about pocket PCs or smartphones, visit Pocket PC Central at pocketpccentral.net, which demystifies the hardware and its capabilities in Plain English.

Minding the Store

Although you're still in the early stages of planning your new salon/spa, it's not too soon to start thinking about some of the specific operational issues that will impact and contribute to the success of your business. To begin with, you must consider your hours of operation carefully so you can accommodate the maximum number of clients during the business day. You undoubtedly already know that the beauty business isn't a 9-to-5 kind of industry. With the exception of urban businesses, which close up when the office workers go home, salons generally are open seven days a week and on some of the traditional holidays, and their hours may be extended around prom time or during peak wedding season. Even day spas usually are open on Sundays since this often is the only time during the week that a busy professional or mom can get away for some personal pampering.

Typically, hair salons in metropolitan areas are open from 10 A.M. to 9 P.M. seven days a week and from 10 A.M. to 6 P.M. in smaller communities. By design, Sunday and holiday hours often are the same as those of local retailers like malls and department stores, and generally run from noon to 5 P.M. Lunch hours and early evening hours tend to be the busiest times for salons. You also may need to have special hours to accommodate special needs. For example, if you do a lot of wedding work, you'll probably have to be open earlier on Saturday mornings, say at 7 A.M., for the brides who have to get to church for a 10 A.M. service.

Beware!
Make sure you don't undercharge for services, even if you have a low break-even point. You'll be so booked up that you won't be able to fit in new clients, and your business won't be able to grow.

The Price Is Right

Another important part of your salon development plan is the appropriate pricing of your services. Set prices too high, and you'll limit the number of people who can afford them; set them too low, and you'll limit your profit potential, and possibly put the business at risk. Of course, the price the market will bear is very much dependent on the demographics of your service area. If you're in an upscale area with larger homes occupied by people with more disposable income, you can price your services accordingly, and even offer high-end spa services. But if the surrounding community is peopled by young working families, you'll have to forego the spa services (or offer no more than the bare minimum) and concentrate instead on basic haircutting, affordably priced color services, and manicures.

Setting prices requires more than visiting other salons in your target market, collecting service menus, and pricing your own services so they're competitive. Rather, you must consider the three factors that will influence your prices: labor and supplies, overhead, and profit.

Labor costs for salons/spas include salary and benefits costs for both your stylist/spa staff and administrative people (including your manager, receptionist, and other support staff). Your own salary is included as a part of this cost. This cost is generally expressed as a price per hour and can vary depending on the amount of time it takes your employees to cut hair or perform other services.

According to the Bureau of Labor Statistics' (BLS) most recent *Occupational Outlook Handbook*, half of all salaried hairdressers, hairstylists, and cosmetologists earn an average of $21,320 per year (including tips and commissions). Based on a 40-hour week, that works out to $10.25 per hour. On the other hand, a survey by the National Accrediting Commission of Cosmetology Arts and Sciences says the average total income for a stylist in a full-service salon (excluding tips) is $40,000 a year, or $19.23 per hour. That's quite a wide spread, so you will need to find out how much salons in your area are paying so you can come in at the appropriate rate.

Here's a way to figure out your costs. Using the lower $10.25 per hour rate mentioned above, assuming it takes a stylist 45 minutes to shampoo, cut, and style one customer, and assuming that materials constitute 6 percent of labor cost, your labor and materials cost would work out like this:

Time		Rate	Cost
Labor	45 min.	$10.25/hour	$7.70 (rounded up from $7.69)
Benefits (15% of labor*)			1.16
Total labor cost			$8.86
Materials (6% of total labor cost)			.53
Total labor/materials cost			**$9.39**

*According to the U.S. Department of Labor, in 2009, benefits comprised 29.2 percent of total employee compensation. Salons typically pay 15 to 25 percent, so we're using that figure here instead.

Next, you need to consider your overhead costs, which consist of all costs required to operate the business other than labor. This includes your mortgage or lease payment, utilities, and so on. Since you don't have prior-year expense data to base this figure on, it's reasonable to estimate that your overhead will be from 40 to 50 percent of your labor and materials cost. (This figure can be adjusted later as you accumulate financial data.)

So let's say when you tally up all your labor and materials costs for the year, you arrive at a figure of $100,000. Your estimated overhead expenses (at 45 percent) would be $45,000. This would give you an overhead rate of 45 percent. Using that overhead rate, you can calculate your operating expenses as:

> ## Bright Idea
>
> To increase your visibility and build goodwill in the community, you can donate professional services (like a haircut and styling or a massage) or a basket of beauty products to key charitable organizations for fundraisers or raffles. Just don't overextend yourself—make sure you can afford the gift in terms of time and cost.

Labor/materials cost	$9.39
Overhead (45% of $9.39)	4.23
Subtotal of operating expenses	**$13.62**

The last part of the pricing equation is profit. Salon owners generally can expect to have a net profit of 11 to 15 percent (although you can certainly make this profit figure higher or lower as you see fit). To arrive at the net profit you want, you have to add a markup percentage factor so you'll arrive at the approximate gross amount you'll earn. We've provided a markup table on pages 17–18 to help you.

Let's assume you want to net a profit of 15 percent. To determine a basic haircut price, use this equation:

Subtotal of operating expenses	$13.62
Net profit	2.41
(17.7% of $13.62)	
Basic cut/style price	**$16.03**

Obviously, many salons charge far more than this amount for a basic cut/style— usually more like $30 to $40—and in these cases, their costs are covered and their net profit is secure. In fact, Neil Ducoff, founder of Salon Business Strategies in Centerbrook, Connecticut, says he knows one stylist who can do a $90 haircut in seven minutes—and does it well.

John Palmieri of Scizzors in Shrewsbury, Massachusetts, simplifies the process of setting prices to the extreme. He suggests figuring out how much the salon needs to

Markup Table

Net Profit Percent of Price	Markup Percent of Cost	Net Profit Percent of Price	Markup Percent of Cost
4.8	5.01	25	33.3
5	5.3	26	35
6	6.4	27	37
7	7.5	27.3	37.5
8	8.7	28	39
9	10	28.5	40
10	11.1	29	40.9
10.7	12	30	42.9
11	12.4	31	45
11.1	12.5	32	47.1
12	13.6	33.3	50
12.5	14.3	34	51.5
13	15	35	53.9
14	6.3	35.5	55
15	17.7	36	56.3
16	19.1	37	58.8
16.7	20	37.5	60
17	20.5	38	61.3
17.5	21.2	39	64
18	22	39.5	65.5
18.5	22.7	40	66.7
19	23.5	41	70
20	25	42	72.4
21	26.6	42.8	75
22	28.2	44.4	80
22.5	29	46.1	85
23	29.9	47.5	90
23.1	30	48.7	95
24	31.6	50	100

Markup Table, continued

Net Profit Percent of Price	Markup Percent of Cost	Net Profit Percent of Price	Markup Percent of Cost
52.4	110	66.7	200
54.5	120	69.2	225
56.5	130	71.4	250
58.3	140	73.3	275
60	150	75	300
61.5	160	76.4	325
63	170	77.8	350
64.2	180	78.9	375
65.5	190	80	400

make for the year and do the math to arrive there. For instance, let's assume you want the salon to make $75,000 per year. Here are the calculations you'd use to figure out your prices:

$75,000/52 weeks = $1,442 per week

$1,442/100 hours the salon is open each week = $14.42/hour

Add a 10 percent profit margin ($1.42) = $15.84/hour

"And when any of your costs go up, you just adjust your hourly rate to cover them," he adds.

Palmieri says this formula works for him because all services basically cost the same amount per hour. Also, having a set rate like this prevents problems, such as having specialists like colorists earning more, or worrying about the cost for products (which are worked into the formula at a rate of 7.5 percent anyway).

"It really makes everything easier," he says. "Why drive yourself crazy?"

All the formulas described here for pricing haircuts can be used for pricing all other salon and spa services.

At Their Service

Next on your initial list of things to do should be to create a salon services menu. This should be handled as soon as you determine exactly which services you'll offer and how you'll price them, since your menu can be given out to potential clients or used as a direct-mail piece to generate pre-opening buzz about the business. Ultimately, you should display a quantity of these menus in a holder on your reception desk so they're always nearby for customers who are interested in other services.

The salon services menu is usually formatted as a brochure. It should reflect the look you want for your salon, from high style to snazzy, funky to cool. Ideally, it should be printed in the same colors as your salon is decorated, and on the best stock you can afford, like 75-pound enamel cover stock (a type of shiny card stock that can be printed in vibrant colors).

You also might consider having a graphic designer create a logo for your salon, which can be used on your menu, salon sign, promotional materials, business cards, and other printed pieces. It should have a distinctive look so it can stand alone without having the name of your salon with it. Examples of logos that do this successfully are the Nike "swoosh" and Microsoft Windows' flying window emblem, both of which effectively evoke their product brand when you see them.

The copy on the menu should be simple but descriptive enough so that clients know what each service entails. For instance, there's no mystery when it comes to a description like "blow dry and style" or "spa manicure." But "dimensional special effects" might not be as obvious, and since some people are too embarrassed to admit they don't understand, they'll never be a consumer of that particular service since they don't have a clue what it is. You'll find a sample salon services menu on page 22.

If you're opening a spa, you really have to be descriptive and creative when it comes to your services menu because so many of the services may not be familiar to the average salon customer. Even people who have been to a spa may be unfamiliar with a term like "parafango therapy" (a combination of paraffin and mud often used to decrease the appearance of cellulite) or a service like "salt glow exfoliation" (which uses mineral salts, often from the Dead Sea, to exfoliate and rejuvenate skin). In Chapter 8, you'll find descriptions of spa treatments that will be helpful when you write your own spa menu copy.

If you've decided to offer spa services as a way to increase revenue and emulate the level of service offered at fine spa resorts, you should describe these services in detail on your spa menu. As a way to build excitement and interest, try trotting out all the adjectives your third grade English teacher told you to lock away for good. For instance, the following adjectives could be used to describe a facial: deep-cleansing, deluxe, purifying, rejuvenating, anti-aging, refining, and refreshing.

Even though you want your salon and/or spa menu to look classy, you don't necessarily have to spend a fortune printing it. To save money on printing costs, have it designed as an 8½-by-11-inch document that can be folded into a two-panel brochure size (which fits a standard No. 10 envelope). Also, the more pieces you print, the lower the per-piece price will be. Just be sure you don't print too many at a time since prices and services do change.

Swabbing the Decks

Another operational task that's required to uphold the image of your salon is regular maintenance. It's not enough to sweep up hair clippings after a cut or to wash and fold towels—you have to keep the salon looking and smelling fresh and clean so it's inviting at all times, no matter how much traffic comes through the door or how bad the weather is. Some salon owners prefer to have a maintenance crew come in to handle everything except the basics like sweeping and folding towels. The cost can be high, at up to $200 per visit, but the benefits truly do outweigh the cost. Alternatively, you could hire a person whose job is to clean up, do laundry, and otherwise keep the salon tidy. Scizzors' John Palmieri has a full-time maintenance employee on staff who arrives two hours before the salon opens to do the laundry, sweep, clean up the refreshment center, and fold towels, among other chores. "That way, we have a very clean salon, which is important. We're all just too busy to clean up after ourselves," Palmieri says.

The majority of owners interviewed for this book simply make daily maintenance, from vacuuming to taking out the trash and dusting counters, a responsibility of every person in the salon. "That's the benefit of a team-based employment system," says Daryl Jenkins of HairXtreme in Chester, Virginia. "It doesn't matter if you're cutting hair or folding towels—everyone is expected to pitch in. The only other help we have is a floor guy who comes in every two weeks to do the floors and carpet at a cost of $55 per visit."

To find a company that offers daily, weekly, or monthly maintenance contracts, check the Yellow Pages under Janitorial Service.

Magic Money Makers

How would you like to help your salon make extra money each month with very little effort? Then plan to offer a carefully selected assortment of retail hair-care and spa products.

According to industry experts, retail products can make your profits grow significantly. Other than ordering the product, arranging it attractively on shelves in your reception area, rotating product, and controlling inventory, there's not much more involved in product retailing. But you do have to educate your staff to sell the products they use on their clients, you have to make the products easily accessible in the salon, and you have to sell a wide enough assortment of products to appeal to most—if not all—customers.

Since your stylists and spa technicians are the best salespeople for retail products, you can pump up retail sales by offering them a performance bonus for selling a certain dollar amount of retail products each month or quarter. Or you could tie their annual merit raises to sales goals you set at the time of their annual performance evaluation.

To increase product visibility in the salon/spa, display hair-care products like shampoo, conditioner, mousse, gel, and wax, as well as implements like brushes, combs, and dryers, prominently in the reception area, preferably on the wall that faces the chairs where clients wait. Don't pack the shelves too tightly, or it will discourage the casual looker from picking up products and reading their labels. Finally, make sure you offer a wide enough selection of products. This is especially important if you decide to specialize in just one product line, like Aveda or Bumble and bumble. Clients will expect to see every product necessary to tame their tresses and keep them looking salon-fresh.

Salon Equipment International, which keeps its finger on the pulse of salon and spa industry issues, says that retail sales should account for 25 percent of a salon's overall profits. So you can see there's a lot of money to be made if employees are trained correctly, and you have the right products on hand. Among the product lines the salon owners interviewed for this book feature in their salons are Aveda, Bumble and bumble, and Goldwell. See the Appendix for contact information for some of the industry's leading professional salon product manufacturers.

The Gift of Beauty

One aspect of salon sales that has really heated up recently is gift certificate sales. Many salons offer either paper gift certificates or plastic gift cards as a way to corral more cash during those all-important gift-giving seasons, like the December holiday period, Valentine's Day, and Mother's Day. Many of the owners interviewed for this book are making big bucks on gift certificate sales—$200,000 a year in the case of one salon/spa that has annual revenues of $3 million; $170,000 a year at another salon/spa that has annual sales of just under $1 million. On the other hand, another owner says gift certificate sales are minimal because the salon doesn't have spa services. What appears to be more typical is a gift certificate sales rate of about 10 percent of overall sales.

The beauty of gift certificates is that they bring in a lot of cash for a very small investment. If you're lucky, many of your gift certificates will be redeemed during the slower months that follow the holiday gift-giving season. If you're even luckier, the

Salon Services

Cutting and Styling		Permanent Wave	
Design cut and style	$45 to $65	Permanent wave without cut	$75 and up
Blow dry and style	$25	Spiral perm without cut	$150 and up
Hot roller set	$35	Permanent wave with cut	$115 and up
Evening updo	$40 and up	Spiral perm with cut	$190 and up
Conditioning	$25	Spot perm	$50 and up

women who receive gift certificates for Mother's Day will come in during the slower summer months. But don't leave anything to chance—be sure to budget the initial gift certificate purchase money wisely so you'll easily be able to handle the increased operational costs that could result when they're redeemed. And, of course, there's always the chance that gift certificates can be lost or misplaced, but in these cases, you're covered: You've made money without having to spend money on labor and materials.

Daryl Jenkins of HairXtreme has some blunt advice for salon owners thinking of starting a gift card program. "Go with an electronic gift card system," he says. "Handling paper was insane." Besides being time-consuming to fill out, paper gift certificates are more complicated to track. It's also easier to lose them—and for the consumer to duplicate them fraudulently. Encoded cards are pretty much error-free.

Finally, Gift Card USA (giftcardusa.com), a provider of plastic gift cards and loyalty programs, says customers spend 40 percent more with plastic gift cards than with paper, which is why virtually all large retailers use them. Research has shown that gift cards also improve client loyalty and retention.

Smart Tip

Tip...

To increase retail sales, try creating small hair-care product displays at each stylist station. Although these mini displays should focus mainly on the products each stylist uses at his/her station, you certainly can include other new or innovative products as part of the mix.

To implement a gift card program, you'll need a plastic card printer/encoder for magnetic stripe cards, a handheld scanner or a magnetic strip reader, and a supply of plastic gift cards. Typical costs for a gift card program include setup, monthly and transaction fees; the cost of supplies (including the cards and display materials); and a fee to buy or lease the equipment. You'll find the names of a few gift card program vendors you can explore in the Appendix.

Casting Your (Hair)net: Market Research

The last time you were in the market for a new car, did you walk into the dealership nearest your house, point at the car parked inside the door, and pay the sticker price without a thought about your budget? Probably not. Instead, you likely checked out what other people were driving, carefully researched the vehicles you wanted on the internet or in showrooms, asked friends and business associates for recommendations, and then checked *Consumer Reports* or other sources before taking a test drive. Then you signed on the dotted line.

Although choosing a new hair salon isn't as risky for consumers as making a new vehicle purchase, and hair care costs much less than automobiles, your prospects are likely to choose just as carefully. Their decision will be based on the salon's reputation, recommendations from friends, location, and of course, price. And since you don't have a reputation yet, it's your job to get the word out about the great products and services you're going to offer so customers will want to patronize your salon. Market research will help you do this efficiently and successfully.

Dollar Stretcher

The U.S. Census Bureau's website (census.gov) has a wealth of demographic information available by state and county that can be useful when you're doing your market research. Most of the information is available online at no charge, which is easy on the budget.

Before we plunge into the wonderful world of marketing, please note that market research is not the same as advertising (which we'll discuss in Chapter 11). By market research, we mean the process you go through to identify the people you want to service, and the plan you'll develop to entice them to visit your salon. And take heed, young Jedi: You must not bypass this step, or the Force will not be with you. All the clever and expensive advertising in the world won't attract customers and increase your bottom line if you're marketing to the wrong audience.

Market research does all the following things:

- It helps you identify exactly who might be interested in using your services.
- It helps you determine whether the geographical area in which you want to set up shop can actually sustain your new salon/spa.
- It provides you with useful information and data that can help you avoid big problems down the road that could negatively impact your business (i.e., problems that could put you out of business).

You might be thinking, "I went to cosmetology school to avoid taking a statistics class! Besides, there are heads everywhere, and many have bad haircuts. They'll flock to my door." You hope. The truth is, although the beauty industry is a nearly $46 billion business, according to IBISWorld, a provider of industry intelligence and information, not every neighborhood nor every part of the country has the same need for salon services. Take, for instance, the two-block stretch in Baltimore where, in a recent year, ten hair-care salons were doing business, according to Vander Harris Jr., former president of the National Black Hair Association. That's probably not an optimal place to start another new salon. Or consider parts of Florida where retirement homes dot the landscape like dandelions in spring. You probably wouldn't want to establish a trendy, high-end salon that offers spiral perms and French manicures when the local populace is more interested in roller sets and basic permanent waves.

The best way to find out about these kinds of shortcomings—as well as the potential opportunities—is by doing some research on your target market. This is something you can do yourself without too much difficulty even if your schooling didn't include a single course in statistics or research.

"With the exception of questionnaire development, which can be difficult for a beginner to do well, you can pretty much handle all the research by yourself on a reasonably small budget," says David L. Williams, dean of the School of Business Administration and a professor of market research at Wayne State University in Detroit. "The problem is, many small-business owners view market research as an optional expense. But it's the only accurate way you have to find out what's important to your customer."

And since profits and a successful business are what's important to you, let's get started.

Finding Clients to Dye For

If you watch late night TV, you might have seen an obscure movie called *Suppose They Gave a War and Nobody Came*. So just imagine what it would be like if you opened a stylish, well-equipped salon and nobody came. It could happen if you don't identify your target market before you open your front door.

Although the formula for defining your target audience may seem simple (People + Hair = Hair Salon Clients), the reality is that there's a lot more to starting a hair salon than putting your entire life savings on the line and stocking up on shampoo. That's why you need to start the market research process by carefully analyzing the demographics of the area where you plan to do business so you can tailor your services to a specific group within that market.

Demographics are defined as statistics about or characteristics of your target audience that make them likely to use your services. Among the characteristics important for salon owners are age, gender, education, occupation, income level, and geographic location. A savvy owner-to-be will consider ways to reach several of these demographic segments at the same time.

Here's an example: Let's say your dream is to open a salon in the small university town where

Tip...

Smart Tip
If you're cyber-challenged, try contacting your state's department of commerce or finance, or the local university, for census or demographic information that can help in your market research. Larger libraries also may have hard copies of Census Bureau materials.

you grew up. You want to offer upscale, trendy hair and nail services in spacious, elegantly appointed surroundings. Part of the plan is to convert a section of the facility at a future date into a fashionable day spa that offers hydrotherapy and Scotch hose treatments, but in the meantime you'll just turn that area into a charming French bistro and serve flavored coffee and healthy snacks. The only location you can afford that has enough room for all your

Stat Fact

According to the recent Economic Census, California has the most hair salons with 6,121. Florida is in second place with 5,470, and New York ranks third with 5,467.

planned services and future expansion is in a once-thriving strip mall on the outskirts of Universityville that's bordered by a middle-class community of 1950s-era bungalow homes. Many of the families living there have young children and one wage-earner.

The question is, Can your salon survive there? Test your instincts by choosing an answer in this mini quiz:

A. Maybe not, because university students may not be able to afford upscale salon services.
B. No, because the single-earner families spend all their disposable income on Happy Meals and soccer camp.
C. Absolutely not, because the strip mall is in a lousy location.
D. All of the above.

The best answer is D. If you only had one of these pre-existing conditions to deal with, you might be able to make a go of it. But combine all of them, and they turn into a noxious brew simmering with potentially lethal consequences. But if you were to open that same salon in an upscale community near, say, an Ivy League university, your chances of success would rise a notch. If there's a country club nearby, that's a plus. If the median age of women in the community exceeds 30 and they're white-collar professionals, so much the better. Add it all together, and you've improved your chances of success significantly. Then all you have to do is make sure your salon services are top-notch and the business generates positive buzz in the community (two things that are under your control).

Lorinda Warner and her partner (now retired) wisely considered demographics when they opened Lorinda's Salon Spa Store in Mill Creek, Washington, in 1984. "We knew where we wanted to be based on growth in our area and a new high-end planned golf course community," says Warner. "We backed up our decision with traffic counts and income information from the local chamber [of commerce]. We also had a cheap, anchored, and nicely-shaped strip mall location."

The Tao of Economics

All this talk of demographics is fine and dandy, but the main thing that will influence business in your salon will be economics. After all, when the national economy is riding high, people are willing and able to spend money on more expensive salon services like texturizing, services that can easily be done at home like beard trimming, and luxury spa services like full-body massage and body wraps. But when the economy is slumping, those services may be considered a luxury rather than a necessity. As a result, customers may cut back on the frequency of their salon visits, or they may opt only for the basic services provided by one of the budget-conscious national hair care chains.

One way to avoid being caught up a creek without an applicator is to research your target market's economic base carefully. If you've done your market research well so far, you already have some idea of the average income levels in your neighborhood. Now you need to look at data like the percentage of people who are employed full time and the types of jobs they hold. If the local market is driven by a lot of blue-collar, heavy industry jobs, a downturn in the economy could make cash tight and affect your ability to keep customers. So could a plant shutdown or a scaling back of local services. Luckily, most people still do use salon services, even if it's just for a basic cut, when times are tough, but they may go longer between services. So make a phone call to your city's economic development office now to get a handle on the health of local industry.

While you're at it, ask about the area's white-collar jobs and the types of companies that support them. Be wary if the local economy is heavily supported by just one industry, like high-tech or beet farming. Chances are, the economy of the entire area has the potential to go south in an economic downturn (or a drought), taking your prospective customers with it. If you decide that's where you want to locate anyway, make sure you have a backup survival plan if the worst happens.

Judy Rice Mangum of Goldwaves Salon & Spa in Fort Worth, Texas, didn't do any research when she started her salon in 1988, but when her daughter, Leslie Rice, came aboard as marketing director in 2000, all that changed. "I wrote a six-month plan back then that was a combination game plan, advertising plan, and promotion budget," says Rice. "Now I review it every month so we always know where we're going."

Dollar Stretcher

The Yellow Pages can be a great source of information about your competition since it lists the salons in operation in your area and their precise locations. Try doing a little research in both the hard copy directory and the online version at yellowpages.com.

Debbie Elliott of Debbie Elliott Salon & Day Spa in Portland, Maine, didn't have a marketing plan at startup either, but realizes she should have. "I didn't know what a SWOT (strength, weakness, opportunity, and threat) analysis was. I just had more of a feeling about what would work, although that's not very scientific," Elliott admits. "But now I update my marketing plan every six to nine months and look at it frequently in between. A good marketing plan can help a salon that's growing comfortably do even better."

Angela Marke of Andrew Marké Salon in Macomb, Michigan, got her initial marketing research assistance from an unexpected source: the strip mall's management office. The leasing agent sent demographics and other information that indicated that on a demographic scale of 1 to 10, her location was rated 10. Part of the reason is that the strip mall has a large grocery store as its anchor, which gives Marke a lot of walk-in traffic.

So the bottom line is that although it's possible to launch a new salon without doing much (or any) market research and still make it work, your chances of success are greater if you take the time to develop a detailed marketing plan.

Conducting Market Research

There are two types of research. Primary research is information gathered firsthand from people in response to written or verbal questions, while secondary research is garnered by studying information gathered by other researchers. Both can yield useful information for formulating your marketing strategy.

Primary research comes in three flavors relevant to salon owners: historical, observational, and survey. With historical research, you rely on past data to make inferences about your market. An example of this would be checking business records to determine the failure rate for salons in your market. Observational research consists of observing your potential customers to determine their buying behaviors and other criteria. You could try sitting in the main courtyard of the mall outside a salon and observing how its customers use salon services and buy products. Or you can check the parking lot of a nearby salon at various times of the day to assess traffic flow. But strive to notice the little things as you watch, like a customer's frustration at having to wait for the receptionist, or you'll be just like Dr. Watson in the story *A Scandal in Bohemia*, about whom Sherlock Holmes remarked, "You see, but you do not observe."

As a prospective salon owner, you may find that surveys are your best source of primary research information. The three most common types of surveys are direct mail, telemarketing, and personal interviews. Owners of startup businesses often find direct-mail surveys to be the most cost-effective and least time-consuming technique for gathering information. They're also easy to produce and send out to the prospect list you identify.

To save money for other startup costs, like equipment and advertising, you should consider doing the survey yourself rather than hiring a marketing research firm. The survey should be no more than one page long since it's difficult to get busy people to fill out anything lengthier. The questions should be well phrased so they're short, direct, and clear. They also should be constructed so the information they gather is useful and conducive to analysis. For example, a question like "Would you be interested in services like facials?" isn't very useful because it's closed-ended, meaning it's possible for the respondent to give a yes or no answer without elaborating. That's not going to give you much insight, which is the whole point of this exercise. A better way to phrase the question might be, "How many times last year did you have a facial?"

Tip...

Smart Tip

Big companies make a huge investment in market research, which is why they have a distinct advantage over smaller companies that provide the same products or services. Market research allows you to identify trends and formulate better ways to reach particular market segments. So for marketing success, do as the big boys do and collect marketing information on a regular basis.

While you shouldn't have too much trouble compiling the results of your survey and analyzing the data, you might find it helpful to have the questions written by someone experienced in market research. But because market research firms tend to be pricey, Williams at Wayne State University suggests contacting the business school at your local university instead. A marketing professor in the school of business administration might be willing to draft your questionnaire for $500 to $1,000, or may even assign your questionnaire as a class project free of charge, as Williams himself has done. In the meantime, you'll find a sample cover letter and market research questionnaire on pages 32, 33, and 34 that you can use as a guideline.

Gathering Cutting-Edge Information

Once you have your survey in hand, you're ready to mail it out to a random sampling of consumers in your area. The easiest way to do this is to purchase a mailing list that's targeted to the market you're interested in. Local homeowners' associations, list brokers, and even daily newspapers in major metropolitan areas can sell you a list of heads of household that can be sorted in many ways, such as by zip code (which allows you to target a specific geographic area) or by profession. In addition, you can find a huge list of publications that sell their lists in the Standard Rate and Data Service directory, published by VNU Business Media, or the Encyclopedia of Associations (Gale Research), both of which can be found in many large libraries.

8565 Park Avenue
Lincoln Park, Michigan 48146
(313) 555-1212
edmundstanley.com
info@edmundstanley.com

July 5, 201x

Ms. Venisa Lalik
46 Spring Lake Road
Allen Park, Michigan 48101

Dear Ms. Lalik:

Please accept as our gift the enclosed $5 gift certificate toward any service valued at $75 or more at the new Edmund Stanley Salon & Spa, debuting in Lincoln Park on September 6.

A visit to Edmund Stanley will enhance your natural beauty and refresh your spirit. You'll experience complete hair and beauty renewal services proffered by expert stylists and color specialists in a setting of luxury and elegance. Or you can luxuriate in the comfort of our Zen-like grotto while experienced aestheticians pamper you and enhance your inner beauty.

Edmund Stanley Salon and Spa is located in the King's Pointe Plaza at 8565 Park Avenue in Lincoln Park. Please plan to join us there for a grand opening celebration on Saturday, September 6, from 10 A.M. to 2 P.M. Until then, please let us know how we can best serve your beauty and aesthetics needs by answering the following questions and returning your completed survey to us. A postage-paid envelope is enclosed for your convenience.

We look forward to serving you soon.

Very truly yours,

Edmund Stanley

Edmund Stanley
Master Stylist and Owner

Salon and Spa Guest Questionnaire

Edmund Stanley Salon & Spa Guest Questionnaire

1. Where do you presently have your hair cut and styled (salon name)?

   _____

2. How often do you use salon services?
   ❏ Weekly ❏ Monthly ❏ Other (specify) _____

3. How much do you pay for cut/style services? _____

4. Have you ever visited a day spa before?
   ❏ Never ❏ 1–2 times ❏ 3+ times

5. Which of the following spa treatments have you tried? (check all that apply)
   ❏ Facial ❏ Spa manicure/pedicure ❏ Massage ❏ Hydrotherapy
   ❏ Body wraps ❏ Aromatherapy ❏ Exfoliation ❏ Manual lymph drainage

6. Which spa services would you most wish to try? (check all that apply)
   ❏ Facial ❏ Spa manicure/pedicure ❏ Massage ❏ Hydrotherapy
   ❏ Body wraps ❏ Aromatherapy ❏ Exfoliation ❏ Manual lymph drainage

7. What is your age?
   ❏ 18–29 ❏ 30–45 ❏ 46–60 ❏ 61 and up

8. Which of the following are important to you when it comes to using salon/spa services? (check all that apply)
   ❏ Price ❏ Extended salon hours ❏ Stylists' training
   ❏ Online booking capability ❏ Wide selection of retail products

9. Are you satisfied with the services offered at your current salon?
   ❏ Yes ❏ No
   If not, why not?_____

Salon and Spa Guest Questionnaire, continued

10. Would you be interested in receiving an e-newsletter or following us on Twitter, where we highlight salon and spa products and monthly specials?
    ❑ Yes ❑ No
    If yes, please provide your e-mail or Twitter address:

    _____

11. What is your household income?
    ❑ $25,000 and under ❑ $25,001–$40,000 ❑ $40,001–$55,000
    ❑ $55,001–$70,000 ❑ $70,001 and up

12. What is your educational level?
    ❑ High school diploma ❑ College degree ❑ Graduate school degree

13. What is your profession? _____

Some other criteria to explore that might be of value to a salon owner include gender (since women tend to use more personal care services than men), income (which helps to determine whether your market can support upscale services like massage and hydrotherapy), and age (professional women and baby boomer women are frequent salon service consumers). The average price to rent a consumer list is $140 per 1,000 names, according to list manager Worldata, but regional lists often go for much less. The lists usually are available on CD, and you can print your own pressure-sensitive labels if you plan to mail that way. If you don't want to survey that many people, remove every nth label (as in 4th or 10th) or delete records from the master list until you get the number you want.

Another good source of "hot lists," or lists with names of proven buyers, is beauty industry shows. The organizations that run these trade

Smart Tip

Compiled lists are lists of names that have been gathered from a variety of published lists, including telephone directories and organization rosters. *Hot* lists consist of the names of known buyers and are usually taken from magazine subscription lists, mail order buyer lists, and so on. Hot lists cost more to rent but are well worth it because the information is usually more current and accurate.

Tip...

shows usually compile the names of attendees for their exhibitors. You may be able to purchase a copy of the list directly from the trade show organizer. You'll find a list of some of the largest salon industry shows in Chapter 10.

When you're ready to produce your questionnaire, you can keep the cost down by using your home computer to create your own letterhead and format the questionnaire. Just be sure to use high-quality paper to reflect the image you want to project for your salon. Then stop by a quick print shop like FedEx Office and have it photocopied, or upload your document and let FedEx Office do the work for you.

Cashing In

You might be surprised to know that receiving just a 1 percent response to a direct-mail piece is enough to drive direct marketers into paroxysms of joy. But if that isn't enough to make you do a little Snoopy dance, then consider enclosing a crisp, new dollar bill with your survey to increase the response. This is a trick direct marketers use to catch readers' attention when they open the envelope, and is meant to be an advance token of thanks to the recipient for taking the time to fill out and return a questionnaire. Although some recipients will simply pocket the cash and gleefully use it as a down payment on a caramel macchiato on the way to work, direct marketing studies have shown that sending even such a small cash honorarium improves the rate of return for direct mail. So it might be worth a try.

But if you're watching your budget, the cash incentive might not be a viable option since Williams says that a survey should be sent to a sampling of at least 300 people if it's going to yield useful data. (After all, a 1 percent return on 300 surveys means only 3 sent back.) You might find it's more beneficial to use your marketing dollars elsewhere.

Phone-y Business

Another type of primary research that can be highly effective is telemarketing. Even though many people have placed their names on the National Do-Not-Call Registry so they're not bothered by telemarketers, there are still plenty of people who would be willing to talk to you about their salon preferences if you call them at a reasonable hour and don't require too much of their time.

What makes telemarketing such a powerful tool is that you can hear feelings and emotions behind the words spoken by the person on the other end of the line. Also, you can ask the people you contact to elaborate on their answers, particularly if they raise concerns about issues you never considered before.

As with surveys, you'll need a strong telemarketing script with short questions (like those on your market research questionnaire) and a good prospect list. Have a blank form ready when you call and fill in the answers as you talk so the information is readily available for interpretation later.

Adding a Personal Touch

Since hair care is a hands-on, face-to-face profession, you might want to consider conducting one-on-one interviews to glean pertinent marketing data. Market research firms abound that can help you draft your survey, conduct the research in a public place like a mall, and then compile the results and present their findings. (Such firms are located in most large cities and are listed in the Yellow Pages under Market Research and Analysis.)

As might be expected, the cost of such services can be steep—a smaller shop might charge as much as $4,000 to $8,000 to conduct 200 to 300 interviews, compile and analyze the results, and prepare a report, according to Williams. But if you're fortunate enough to have a healthy startup budget, you may find the cost is justified when you consider how much you can learn from willing subjects. Giving respondents a cash incentive or a free gift is a common practice to make them willing to speak freely and honestly.

Bright Idea

When you mail out a direct-marketing piece, use postage stamps on the envelopes rather than running the envelopes through a postage meter. This gives your mail the appearance of being personal correspondence and increases the likelihood that the envelope will be opened.

A Secondary Option

If your budget is really tight, you may want to consider using secondary research as the main gizmo in your market research toolbox. Secondary research isn't as complex as primary research; all it requires is knowing where to look to find information that will help you make general marketing assumptions. The internet has made the process of locating useful secondary research a breeze while giving you access to information you might otherwise not have come across.

The world's greatest repositories of statistical information can be found at state and federal agencies since they collect data on everything from educational levels to buying habits. This data isn't always fresh (it's often a year or two old since it takes those big lumbering government machines a while to chug along), but it still can be very useful. Some sources to investigate include the U.S. Census Bureau (census.gov), the SBA (sba.gov), local economic development organizations, and even utility companies, which often have demographic data they'll provide free of charge or for a nominal fee. In addition, your county, borough, or parish usually will allow you to

Beware! When you purchase a mailing list for direct-mail use, you're entitled to use it just once. Since each list is "seeded" with control names, the seller will know if you use it more than once. If you think you'll want to use the list again, you might be able to negotiate a multiple-use discount rate.

view census tracts, which include information about population density and distribution. This can be useful to determine whether the local population is growing, static, or declining—an important consideration when you're thinking about establishing a new business.

Other sources of useful secondary research include your local library, chamber of commerce, trade publications (like *Modern Salon*), and industry associations. (You can find the names of thousands of trade publications in Standard Rate and Data Service.) Also, don't overlook the Yellow Pages as a good source.

The Beauty listings are useful for determining how many salons are operating in your area (since they're all likely to have at least a one-line listing) and where they're located.

Charting Your Course

Understanding your market and the people you'll serve is critical to the success of your business. But understanding yourself and defining who and what you are, as well as exactly what you plan to accomplish as a salon owner, are equally important. So follow the lead of America's most successful corporations, and write a simple mission statement that includes your company's goals and outlines how you'll fulfill them.

A simple mission statement for a hair salon might say, "The Salon at Twelve Oaks will cater to the beauty needs of busy professionals by providing complete hair and nail services in an atmosphere of luxury and serenity. Our goal is to have an active client base of 500 people in the first six months."

Here's another possible approach: "Edmund Stanley Salon & Spa is a full-service facility that offers more services than the three closest competitors combined. Luxury services and amenities, as well as highly trained and experienced stylists and aestheticians, are the hallmarks that will distinguish this business and result in first-year sales of $100,000."

And here are some actual mission statements provided by the salon and spa owners we spoke to:

"Relax, refresh, renew."
—*Hair One Inc., Medford, New Jersey*

Mission Statement Worksheet

Here's your opportunity to try writing your own mission statement. Begin by answering the following questions:

1. Why do you want to start a salon and/or day spa?

_____

_____

2. What are your personal objectives? How do you intend to achieve them?

_____

_____

_____

_____

3. What useful and beneficial skills do you bring to the business?

_____

_____

4. What is your vision for this business? Where do you think you can take it in one, two, and five years?

_____

_____

_____

_____

Using this information, write your mission statement here:

Mission Statement For
(your salon name)

_____

_____

_____

_____

_____

_____

_____

"To have a clean, upbeat, fun, fashion-forward salon with a
high client retention rate and career opportunities
for those who work here."
—*Scizzors, Shrewsbury, Massachusetts*

"Our mission is to provide impeccable world-class services and skills in
a place where clients can feel safe and secure, and think only of
themselves while they're here."
—*HairXtreme, Chester, Virginia*

"Beauty is as much a function of inner tranquility and self-confidence as it
is the presentation of one's positive attributes. It is the dedication to
the client's physical and emotional well-being that always will be
the paramount focus of my professional aspirations."
—*Debbie Elliott Salon & Day Spa, Portland, Maine*

As you can see, mission statements vary in length. The length doesn't matter; the direction the mission statement provides is what's important. Use the "Mission Statement Worksheet" on page 38 to draft your company's mission statement.

Splitting Legal Hairs

Now that you have a good idea whom you'll market your services to, your next step is to create a formal legal framework for your new salon. You should make decisions about your legal form of operation early because the type of organization you create can impact everything from profits to liability, all of which have implications for the viability of your business and its chances of survival.

In general, small businesses like yours usually operate under one of four basic legal forms: sole proprietorship, partnership, corporation, or limited liability company (LLC). Each has its advantages and disadvantages, so a careful study of each type is recommended.

Sole Proprietorship

This is the easiest type of business to form. Under a sole proprietorship, you are the only owner. To open the business, all you have to do is choose a name for your salon, file some paperwork to establish a fictitious name (called a dba, which will be discussed later), obtain a business license, and open a business checking account in the business's new name. You don't need to establish credit in your business's name; rather, you can use your personal credit cards to pay for business expenditures. You'll get tax benefits like business expense deductions, but you don't have to file a separate business tax return. Your income and expenses are simply reported on Schedule C or C-EZ of your personal IRS Form 1040 tax return, and your profits are taxed as ordinary income.

But while there are many benefits to a sole proprietorship, there's a major disadvantage: personal liability. You would be held personally liable for any losses, bankruptcy claims, or legal actions such as malpractice suits that are entered against your business. That can wipe out both your personal and business assets if a catastrophe hits, and given today's litigious society, that's a risk many new salon owners prefer not to take.

The other disadvantage of a sole proprietorship is that it can be difficult to obtain financing from commercial lenders. As a result, you may end up having to risk personal assets anyway to raise enough capital to launch your salon.

Generally speaking, facility-based salons aren't organized as sole proprietorships; they're more likely to be corporations (discussed below). But if you plan to run your salon out of your home, a sole proprietorship is a viable option.

Partnership

If you're planning to join forces with another person or persons to open your salon, you might consider forming a partnership. There are two kinds of partnerships: general partnerships, in which each of the partners participates in the daily running of the business, and limited partnerships, in which one or more general partners run the business while the limited partner(s) supplies working capital but doesn't actively participate in the management of the business.

The advantages of forming a partnership are similar to those of a sole proprietorship. It's easy to set up—all you need is a verbal or written agreement between the partners. (You'll learn later why a written agreement is recommended.) Business profits are divided according to each partner's share of the proceeds and are taxed as personal income. You do have to file a few extra federal forms, which are discussed in IRS Publication 541, *Partnerships*. You can get a copy at your local IRS office or download it from irs.gov.

Like sole proprietorships, the downside of

Smart Tip

If you operate your business under your own name, you can use your social security number when filing your business taxes. But if you adopt another name, or form a partnership or a corporation, you need a Federal Employer Identification Number (EIN). To apply for one, go to irs.gov and search for "EIN." There's no cost to apply, so you don't need to use one of the numerous companies on the internet that charge $49 or more to file for you.

partnerships is related to liability. Each partner is liable for the other's actions (including facing angry creditors when one of the partners skips town after draining the company bank account), and each partner assumes unlimited liability in the event the business is sued or attacked, which again puts both personal and business assets at risk.

If you're interested in setting up a partnership, approach the situation like a formal business transaction even if you've known your partner for years or are related to him/her. It's highly advisable to contact an attorney to draw up an agreement that spells out all the partnership terms, including responsibilities, rights, percentage of business ownership, and so on. That way, if one of you decides to leave the business or you have to dissolve the partnership for any reason (divorce, bankruptcy, relocation, etc.), everything will be clearly defined, and your interests will be protected.

Corporation

The third type of business arrangement is the corporation. It's established as a legal entity totally separate from the business owner and is responsible for its own debts and actions. Keep in mind, however, that it's possible that your creditors or bank will require you to put up personal assets (a car, investments, or even your home) as collateral, so corporations are not necessarily risk-free.

There are two types of corporations. C corporations are the most common form of ownership and offer advantages like limited liability protection, tax benefits for

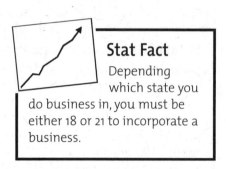

Stat Fact
Depending which state you do business in, you must be either 18 or 21 to incorporate a business.

health and life insurance deductions, and ownership transferability. Their main disadvantage is that profits are taxed twice—first at the corporate tax rate, then again at the personal tax rate (since the owner and all employees are considered employees of the corporation).

S corporations are similar to C corporations but have the tax advantages of partnerships in that the corporation doesn't pay income taxes on profits. Instead, the individual owners pay personal taxes on profits, which reduces the overall tax bite. Obviously, this arrangement sounds a lot better, but along with the tax advantages come a lot of special restrictions and fewer tax deductions. Consult an attorney to help you sort out the pros and cons.

Typically, salon owners choose to incorporate rather than choose one of the other legal forms for their businesses. Establishing a corporation requires filing articles of incorporation, electing officers, and holding an annual meeting. (No need to rent a room at the Hyatt Regency for this purpose—an informal meeting with a written agenda held in the salon will suffice.) The whole process isn't complicated, and you can even incorporate without using an attorney. For instance, LegalZoom.com offers an "Economy" incorporation package for $139 that includes clearing the preliminary corporation name, filing articles of incorporation, creating custom corporate bylaws, and more. Having an attorney handle the process may cost $500 to $700 or more, which in addition to the professional's time covers fees to file the articles of incorporation with the secretary of state (usually $100 to $250), other state filing fees (usually $50 to $200), and more. Incorporation papers are easy to fill out if you want to try to go it alone. However, if your business situation is complex, you probably should consult a corporate attorney. For additional tips and insight into the incorporation process, visit Entrepreneur's website at entrepreneur.com.

Being incorporated has financial implications. First, you'll have to file a business tax return and pay corporate taxes on gross earnings. In addition, you'll still have to file a personal tax return because you're considered an employee of the corporation, even if you're the major or sole stockholder and your salary is taxable. But the good news is that you'll find it easier to obtain financing to buy a building, equip the salon and/or spa, and purchase retail products from beauty suppliers when buying on credit.

Limited Liability Company

The fourth type of business entity is the limited liability company, or LLC. This type of business format combines the tax structure of a partnership yet protects the business owner from personal liability the way a corporation does. It's often compared to the S corporation because of its tax advantages. Your attorney can help you determine whether an LLC is the right legal form for your salon. In fact, it's probably a good idea to consult with an attorney experienced in handling small-business issues right from the start to help figure out which legal form to implement.

"There are advantages to each kind of entity, and an attorney can help you decide which one is best for your situation," says Daniel H. Minkus, a business/corporate attorney in the business practice group of Clark Hill PLC, Detroit. "If you don't know the people you are doing business with, I'd encourage you to form a corporation. They're simple to create, and they're invaluable because your clients are dealing with your enterprise and not you personally."

You'll find information on how to hire an attorney in Chapter 5. And by the way, every salon entrepreneur interviewed for this book chose to incorporate as either a C or an S corporation. The overwhelming reason was that incorporation was the best way to limit their liability.

The Name Game

If you've already thought long and hard about starting your own salon, chances are you've given some thought to choosing a name for it. It's common in the salon industry for owners to select simple, businesslike names that consist of their own names combined with a business description, such as Neelie Lindsay Hair & Nails, or Brendan Alexander Salon. Prefer something more casual? Use just your first name, as in Brittany's Hair Haven.

"My partner [Andrew Bernard] and I ended up combining our names [to come up with Andrew Marké] because the name we wanted had already been taken," says Angela Marke, co-owner of the Macomb Township, Michigan, salon. "The names sounded good together."

Sasha Rash of La Jolie inherited her salon's name, which she promptly pruned to make it sound more contemporary. "La Jolie Coiffeur" had been in Princeton, New Jersey, for 50 years and was popular with the blue-hair roller set when I took it over in 1986," Rash says. "The salon has turned into a wonderful building of fashion, and I dropped the 'coiffeur' because no one could pronounce it and it sounded dated."

Dollar Stretcher

It's easy to do your own no-cost name search using the internet. Start by checking the trademarks registered nationally on the U.S. Patent and Trademark Office website (uspto.gov). You can also search for the name using popular portals like Google, Bing, and Dogpile.

What's in a Name

If you open the Yellow Pages, you'll notice that the names of many of the salons listed under the Beauty heading consist of a person's name with a description of the business (as in Millar Salon Spa Store). But there's no reason why you can't have a clever name like Scizzors (which has worked well for John Palmieri in Shrewsbury, Massachusetts) or Razor's Edge.

"Over the years, I've noticed that the most successful salons have men's names," says Debbie Elliott of Debbie Elliott Salon & Day Spa in Portland, Maine, who chose to use her maiden name as part of her business name despite her observation about the success of salons named after men. "Women's names are often too cute. You want something simple and direct."

Other elements you can incorporate into your salon name include geographical references (Bay Area Snip and Clip) or references to unique local landmarks (Arch House of Beauty would work for a shop in St. Louis, but Death Valley Hair Factory is probably best avoided in California). You also could brainstorm to come up with words related to beauty, hair, and spa, and then see how you can combine them into an evocative name.

Because the hair industry is so creative, fun shop names also abound. John Palmieri, for instance, named his Shrewsbury, Massachusetts, shop Scizzors to emulate the way the word would sound if pronounced phonetically. "And, hey, it was the '80s," he says.

Avoid names that are too cute or could seem outdated as styles change. That means staying away from names that are over the top, like Wild About Hair-y or Nine Inch Nails & Hair. Names like these don't sound professional and won't inspire confidence.

Daryl Jenkins, HairXtreme's vice president of operations, regrets choosing that name for his wife's salon for a number of reasons. "The name sounds like we're into piercing, tattoos, Mohawks, and whacked-out hair," he admits. "We'll do that if you want it, but it's not our niche—we're really more into family hair care. But HairXtreme happened because I tend to be off the wall. For instance, I once wore a goatee with flames in it."

Another thing to consider: selecting a name that starts with a letter that falls at or near the beginning of the alphabet (like A-1 Hair Salon) will put your shop name and phone number near the top of the salon listings in the phone book. This can be helpful for attracting prospective clients who don't have a regular stylist and don't have the inclination to do more than just pick the first salon they see in the telephone directory.

Speaking of the Yellow Pages, when you're considering a salon name, open your local directory to the beauty listings or search online at yellowpages.com to see what other salons in your area are called. If you're in a quiet, upscale neighborhood where the trend is to use the owner's name in the business name, you might want to do the same thing to fit in. On the other hand, you may find that selecting a creative name that bucks the trend could attract more attention.

Once you've picked a suitable name, it's time to move on to the next step: establishing your business identity.

Claiming Your Name

Before you start printing business cards and having a sign made proclaiming your new business name for all to see, there's an important piece of legal business you have to handle. You must register your company name officially to ensure its uniqueness. That's because even if you use your own name in the company name, what you're doing is establishing a fictitious identity, and only one business at a time can have that name. Registration of the new company name is usually done at the county, borough, or parish level by filing a "doing business as" (dba) statement. It will cost you $30 to $60 to file a dba, which entitles you to use the name for a limited period of time, usually three years. When the time expires, you simply renew the dba by paying a fee again.

Before you get permission to operate under your dba, however, a search will be done by the government entity that accepts your application to make sure the name isn't already in use. Name duplication isn't as uncommon as you might think. Just consider how today's common names—Britney, Morgan, Josh, etc.—will become the common salon names of tomorrow. If you happen to choose a name that's already being used, you'll have to pick something else, so it's a good idea to have a couple of names on the back burner.

There are many companies on the internet that would be happy to handle the dba search and filing process for you. However, their fees are exorbitant. Take the dba filing for Carson City, Nevada, for example. One company we know of charges $139 for a dba. But if you go to the Douglas County (Nevada) website, you'll simply download a "Fictitious Name" form and send it in with $20 to obtain your dba, and you'll save $119.

As part of the registration process, you also may have to publish the name in a local newspaper. This varies by state, so ask when you file for your dba. Again, there are internet-based companies that can do this for you for a fee, but it's probably still less expensive to handle this task on your own.

Home-y Pursuits

For the sake of this book, it's assumed you'll be opening your professional salon in a commercial space. But in case you're a prospective salon owner who prefers to start the business in the comfort of your own home (in a legal, taxpaying manner, of course), be aware that there could be local restrictions on such activities. Specifically, your community may have a zoning ordinance that prohibits businesses from operating in residential areas. The idea, of course, is to protect homeowners from excessive traffic and noise, both of which are a distinct possibility when you have salon clients coming and going. It's also highly unlikely that you'll be able to erect a sign on your front lawn.

But if you're really intent on starting a homebased salon, be sure to check with your local government office to see if any special permits are required. It's better to find out upfront, before you go to the expense of installing salon equipment in your basement or den-turned-salon and obtaining a business telephone line, than to find out later that homebased businesses are prohibited in your area.

It's also likely that you'll need a business license to operate a homebased salon, just as a site-based salon does. Such a license is usually available for a nominal fee and is renewable annually. If, by chance, you're turned down for a license because of zoning restrictions, you can apply for (and possibly receive) a variance from the municipal planning commission so you can get your business license. But you'd better go to the commission's meeting prepared to prove that your business won't disrupt the neighborhood. Having an extra-long driveway where clients can park, or providing a written agreement with a nearby commercial business to use some of its parking spaces, would help persuade the powers that be.

> **Beware!**
> Zoning regulations are established at the local level—specifically, the county, borough, parish, city, township, or village level—rather than by the state. A homebased business that's perfectly legal in one city could be *verboten* in another. The only way to find out is by calling the zoning board in your community.

The Business (Plan) of Beauty

Now that you've established your corporate identity, it's time to prepare what undoubtedly will be your salon's most important document: your business plan.

A business plan is like a road map. It outlines your plans, goals, and strategies for making your business successful. It keeps you on track by helping you manage your

salon in the most professional way possible. When done correctly, it also he\
identify your business's strengths and weaknesses. As a result, it must be comp\
well-written, and painfully honest. It also must be fluid and adaptable. Just as h\
styles and the economy change, so must your business plan be adaptable so it can
change to meet current challenges and opportunities in your market.

There's another good reason to have a carefully developed business plan: You'll
need it when you apply for financing or credit at your bank or other financial institution. Most lenders won't even consider a credit application from a business that does-
n't have a comprehensive business plan. Your business plan will demonstrate to
lenders that you're serious about your new salon and have a viable plan to make it successful. Think about it now so you can start putting ideas on paper that can help you
develop and grow your new salon.

There are seven major components every business plan should have. Here's how
these components apply to a hair salon:

1. *Executive summary*. As the name implies, this section summarizes your entire
   business plan. It should include a description of the nature of your business,
   the scope of the services you offer (including brief details about the hair and
   spa services you'll offer, the retail products you'll sell, and so on), the legal
   form of operation you've selected, and your goals. If you'll be using your business plan to seek financing for your salon, you should include details about
   those plans, too.

2. *Business description*. In this section, you present background information about
   both the beauty industry and your target market.
   Chapter 1 of this book has general statistics about the beauty and salon industry
   that may be helpful (although you may
   need to obtain more updated stats), and
   the internet is an invaluable source of
   industry information. The SBA's website
   (sba.gov) is an excellent place to look for
   information that can prove helpful in
   establishing the viability of your business.

3. *Market strategies*. Here's where all that
   market research data you looked up after
   reading Chapter 3 will come in handy. In
   this section, your mission is to analyze
   exactly what you'll do to reach prospective
   clients and how you'll do it. Focus, too, on
   anything that makes your company
   unique, from your personal experience as

Stat Fact

Experts say that
a thoroughly
researched business plan will
be about 25 pages long and
can take 300 hours to prepare
(which includes doing the
research, compiling financial
information, conducting surveys, and writing). But the
effort is worth it because a
well-prepared business plan
will keep you on the right
course and help you find the
financing you may need.

a hairstylist or salon manager to the educational level of your stylists or your aesthetician. This is the place to include your marketing plan, which is your road map for marketing your business to attract customers. We'll discuss the components of a marketing plan and effective advertising strategies in Chapter 11.

4. *Competitive analysis.* As mentioned earlier, you need to know how many salons are already in business in your target market area. You can use this information to good advantage in this section. You also should consider other potential competitors, such as department stores or hotels that offer hair, nail, and makeup services. Analyze competitors' strengths and weaknesses, and then contrast them against what you perceive to be your own. Also, don't forget to consider any aspects that make your salon unique and special, like in-house use of a premium hair-care product line, such as Aveda, or extensive training for colorists.

5. *Design and development plan.* In this section, you'll consider how you'll develop market opportunities to help your salon prosper and grow. One way to do this is to create a timetable of objectives that you can refer to as a way of benchmarking your successes, like setting a goal for growing your client base by a certain percentage or improving your retention rate over a certain time period.

6. *Operations and management plan.* This is where you discuss the day-to-day operations of your salon and/or spa. You can use the information in Chapter 2 of this book as a guide for writing this section. Once your plan is completed, you'll want to be sure to update this section periodically to reflect new or expanded services you offer.

7. *Financial factors.* Whether you're planning a four-chair shop or a big-city mega salon, you need to forecast the success of your business. The idea is to keep your business on track, provide a benchmark against which to compare your success, and avoid unpleasant surprises. The single most important document in this section will be your balance sheet, which provides an ongoing tally of how well the salon is doing and whether (oh, happy day!) you can make investments in equipment and personnel, or you have to curtail spending to make payroll and meet other expenses.

If you're like Pat Millar of Millar Salon Spa Store in Clinton, New Jersey, who considers herself an artist rather than a businessperson, the prospect of writing a busi-

ness plan may seem daunting. But navigating the waters of a new s
out a clear-cut plan is like sailing to Scandinavia without a compa;
you won't have any idea whom you're selling your services to (baby
somethings? professional women?) or what they're interested in.
a college student wants will differ dramatically from the request;
set.) So take the time to formalize your business plan now, and then
ically for both inspiration and direction. For a little guidance, use the "Star",
Checklist" below to make sure you've got everything under control before launching
your new salon.

Startup Checklist

Use the following checklist to make sure you haven't forgotten anything when you're in the throes of the early stages of business planning.

- ❏ Select a business name and apply for a dba.

- ❏ Investigate legal business forms or consult an attorney for advice.

- ❏ Apply for an employer identification number if you're forming a corporation or a partnership.

- ❏ Check local zoning regulations if you're planning to be homebased.

- ❏ Apply for a business license.

- ❏ Write a business plan.

- ❏ Write a marketing plan.

- ❏ Consult an accountant regarding financial and tax requirements related to establishing and operating a business.

5

Leaving the Station
Assembling a Team of Business Professionals

Now that you know the basics of establishing a legal form of operation for your business and the licenses and permits you may need to run it, it's time to think about hiring the professionals who will make your business run smoothly.

"Now wait a minute," you might be thinking. "I do my own taxes. I know my way around a balance sheet. I'm in charge here, and I'll run the whole show myself, thank you very much."

And you're right. But while you're captain of the team that guides your business, you're also still a rookie at this business startup stuff, so you need experienced players who can take you into the end zone, where success and profits await you. Among these players will be an attorney, an accountant, an insurance agent, and a computer expert. (You'll also need a small-business-friendly banker on your team, but we'll discuss banking professionals in Chapter 14.)

A professional team of business experts will help you make the right decisions from the start. They'll help you avoid common startup pitfalls, including costly legal and tax blunders. In short, they'll supply you with the kind of management expertise that will help make your business more stable and solid, which is a real plus when it comes to impressing creditors, bankers, and investors (if you one day choose to go that route).

There's another good reason to put some of the more mundane aspects of running the business into the hands of those who know them best. Your time will be better spent on the activities you do best and went into business in the first place to do, like managing the salon and providing salon services. The other services can and should be handled by people who do them for a living. So while it may be hard to let go of those precious startup dollars to engage the services of experienced professionals, do it anyway. It will be one of the smartest moves you'll make in the early stages of setting up your business.

Legal Briefing

Abraham Lincoln reportedly said, "Any lawyer who represents himself has a fool for a client." That goes double for the salon owner who tries to take on the intricacies of the law without an experienced lawyer.

In today's legalistic society, you need a competent attorney who can negotiate leases, read contracts, and represent you if (horrors!) someone decides to sue because of mental anguish over a bad perm ("I did not request the Don King special!") or after a slip-and-fall accident in an ice-covered parking lot that hadn't yet been salted. It's important to establish a relationship with an attorney now, long before you ever need his or her services, so one day you won't find yourself desperately pawing through the Yellow Pages in search of anyone with a law degree because a guy with a subpoena is peering through your front window at you.

But while being sued (or being threatened with a lawsuit) is an unfortunate possibility, it's more likely you'll need an attorney for more mundane reasons, including:

- You want to form a corporation or a partnership.
- You need assistance deciphering the language in a contract.
- You're signing a contract for a lot of money or one that will cover a long period (like a long-term lease on a new salon site).
- You need help with tax planning, loan negotiations, employee contracts, etc.

A lot of people get nervous about engaging the services of an attorney because of the cost involved. But just as attorneys come in all sizes, shapes, and colors, so do their fees, and it really is possible to find one whose fee schedule fits into your budget. To keep costs down, consider hiring someone in a small local firm, like a one- or two-person practice. Lawyers in smaller practices can spend more time with you than big-city lawyers, who may assign your work to a junior (read: less experienced) attorney. Smaller firms also tend to charge less. Attorneys' hourly rates typically run from $100 to $450, with the higher rates being charged by senior partners and/or those who work at larger firms. Geographic location, the experience of the attorney, and his or her area of expertise also can influence the rate.

Attorney Search

Although it's not necessary to become best friends with the attorney who handles your legal work, it's important to find someone who meets your personal needs and expectations and whose strong communication skills make him or her easy to talk to. Here are some general questions you can ask when you interview prospective legal eagles to determine whether she or he has the right stuff to serve your salon:

- ❍ How long have you been practicing?
- ❍ What's your background and experience?
- ❍ What's your specialty?
- ❍ Do you have other salon owners as clients?
- ❍ Will you do most of the work, or will a paralegal or other aide handle the bulk of the work?
- ❍ Is there a charge for an initial consultation?
- ❍ What do you charge for routine legal work?
- ❍ Do you work on a contingency basis?
- ❍ How can I reach you in an emergency?

Some attorneys charge an initial consultation fee, which you should always ask about when you call to set up your first appointment so you'll avoid a nasty surprise later. In addition, you may have to pay your attorney an upfront retainer, which she or he will draw against as work is completed. Others work on a contingency basis, which means they'll take a percentage of any lawsuit settlement that's reached. Still others charge a flat fee for routine work, such as writing letters or setting up a corporation. At this stage of your business startup, the flat-fee arrangement probably would be most advantageous to you and kinder to your budget.

In addition, many attorneys offer startup packages that can be more affordable for the

Dollar Stretcher

You might be able to save money on attorney's fees by contracting for a prepaid legal plan. After paying a small annual fee, you get services such as telephone consultations, letter writing, and contract review by a qualified attorney. The plans also may provide legal representation at a reduced cost. You can find legal networks in the phone directory under Legal Service Plans.

small-business owner. While you often can tailor such packages to meet your needs, they typically include an initial consultation, as well as all activities related to the incorporation or LLC process, including the filing of paperwork with your state and other corporate formalities. You can expect to pay approximately $900 if you're establishing a corporation. A payment plan may be available to help you handle the cost.

Another way to keep your legal costs reasonable is simply by being organized. "Do your own legwork to gather the information you need beforehand, and then limit the number of office visits you make," says Daniel Minkus of the business practice group of Clark Hill PLC in Detroit. "You also should limit the phone calls to your attorney because you'll be charged for those, too."

Save yourself even more money by going online or stopping by your local library to learn a little about business law before you meet with your attorney. Your intent isn't to learn how to practice law; rather, you need to know enough about the concepts of business law so that you don't waste your hard-earned startup dollars learning the basics from your accommodating attorney whose meter starts running the moment you sit down in his or her office.

A final word about fees: While it's true that cost is a limiting factor when you're starting your business, don't select an attorney just because she or he comes cheap. A shiny new attorney right out of law school may be eager, bright, and affordable, but also will be inexperienced. You need someone who's been around the block—or the courtroom, as the case may be—to keep your legal briefs from getting in a twist.

As with any other professional you'll be hiring—from your shop's interior decorator to the draftsperson or architect who will design the salon layout—you need to do your homework to find the right attorney. Probably the best way to find a legal expert is through personal recommendations from other small-business owners, or organizations like the chamber of commerce or your local economic development group. Another easy way to find a lawyer is through attorney referral services, which are located in many counties throughout the United States. You also could visit the American Bar Association website at FindLegalHelp.org for leads to legal resources, or check out the *Martindale-Hubbell Law Directory* at martindale.com for referrals.

Once you're ready to hire an attorney, treat the whole process the same way you'd handle an employment interview. Ask the candidate about his or her education and experience. Inquire about how much experience he or she has dealing with small businesses, and ask for specifics about the work the attorney handles for these clients. (Remember: An attorney won't divulge clients' names or proprietary information, but should be willing to speak in general terms about work done for others.) Ask for the names of references you can contact (and check them later).

Once you've come to terms with an attorney for services, ask for an engagement letter that puts your agreement—including all fees—in writing.

Incidentally, finding an attorney who has represented other hair salon owners is a plus but not a necessity. However, finding an attorney who's genuinely interested in your business and is pleasant to deal with is definitely a requirement.

Money Mavens

While many people are reluctant to shell out their hard-earned dollars on attorney services, they're usually a lot more open to the idea of hiring an accountant. When it comes to financial matters, most people either have it or they don't. Yet you have to know how your business is doing every step of the way, which makes an experienced accountant an indispensable member of your salon management team.

Accountants work like independent contractors—you pay them for exactly the amount of time they actually work and for the services they provide. They'll help you with important tasks like creating profit and loss statements, making financial projections and forecasting cash flow, analyzing whether an expansion or a move is

Tip...

Smart Tip

You can save money on the cost of tax preparation by using an enrolled agent instead of an accountant since they're fully qualified to represent you before the IRS in an audit. Enrolled agents can be found in the Yellow Pages under Accountants or through the directory found on the National Association of Enrolled Agents' website at naea.org.

economically feasible, and setting up accounting systems. (There's salon software that can help with these tasks, too. It's discussed in Chapter 7, and these software programs are included in this book's Appendix.) A good accountant also is invaluable when it comes to tax issues, particularly since tax law is complicated and changes frequently (the IRS issues new tax rulings every two hours of every business day!). Tax issues that might be relevant to a salon owner include knowing the requirements concerning tax withholding on employees' tips, and setting up a simplified employee pension plan (SEP) for yourself and your employees.

There are two types of accountants. Certified public accountants, or CPAs, are college-educated, licensed professionals who had to pass a rigorous certification examination in the state where they do business in order to put those coveted letters after their names. They usually charge more than public accountants, who aren't certified and don't have to be licensed by the state in which they do business. While they may be perfectly capable due to their experience, public accountants usually can't represent you before the IRS if you're called in for an audit. That's why most business experts recommend using only CPAs, whose credentials are universally recognized and respected by others in business (like banks and investors, for instance).

Although it's advisable to leave the major money matters to your financial wizard, you also need to keep an eye on the store, so to speak, on your own. For that reason, you should invest in one of the many accounting software packages on the market. They'll help you crunch numbers, keep financial records, write checks to vendors, and so on. One program to check out is QuickBooks, which is made specifically for small businesses.

When you're ready to choose the right financial pro for your business, ask your attorney, banker, or professionals in the salon or beauty industry for a referral. The American Institute of Certified Public Accountants' branch in your state also can refer you to a qualified number cruncher, or try accountant-finder.com to find a professional accountant near you. As with attorneys, it's usually advisable to select someone who has experience either with small-business clients in general, or salon owners in particular. By the same token, avoid accountants whose specialty is large corporations since they're not likely to be as tuned into the tax and financial situation of a small-business owner.

The *Occupational Outlook* edition, which is published by the BLS, says that the mean wage for individuals in the accounting industry is nearly $35 an hour. However, self-employed

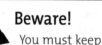

Beware!
You must keep good financial records to stay out of trouble with the IRS. To begin with, be sure to keep receipts for every item you purchase for the salon. If the IRS audits your business, those receipts may be the only thing that stands between you and hefty taxes and penalties.

accountants will charge more, as much as $75 to $125 an hour and up. Organization is definitely the key to keeping your accountant's costs down. Financial records and receipts should be well organized before you meet so you're not paying your accountant top dollar to make neat little stacks of receipts and bills while the clock is ticking. (And if your accounting system has previously consisted of overflowing shoeboxes, get over it now. Invest in a file box with hanging file folders that you can label, and start using it right away.)

You'll find additional bookkeeping strategies and techniques in Chapter 14.

Risk Underwriters

If you've ever had a fender bender or had the local kids mistake your front window for left field, you know the value of good insurance. Ironically, many small-business owners are either underinsured or overinsured. Some try to cut corners when it comes to business insurance, mainly because it costs so much. The problem is, all it takes is one disaster—natural or otherwise—and your entire investment and livelihood could be wiped out. Others are overinsured, often because they make the mistake of trying to buy business insurance from a person whose experience runs to insuring family SUVs or selling life insurance. To avoid both scenarios, you'll want to look for a professional insurance broker who has experience helping small-business owners manage their risk. This is especially important because entrepreneurs like salon owners usually require several types of insurance, which are discussed later in this chapter.

To locate a reputable business insurance broker, turn again to your attorney, accountant, or local business owners for recommendations. You also could contact one of the beauty industry trade associations (quite a few are listed under Associations in the Appendix) to find out whether it has an approved list of insurance brokers. Alternatively, you can find agents listed in the phone book in the Business subcategory of the Insurance listings. As with attorneys and accountants, it's important to interview prospective brokers face-to-face to find the one who best understands the concerns of small-business owners (and ideally, salon owners) and who would be pleasant and accommodating to work with. And don't be shy about comparison shopping for the best price since insurance policy costs can vary widely. Costs

Dollar Stretcher

Using an insurance broker may help you save a significant amount of money on your commercial insurance. Rather than representing only one company, independent agents can recommend the policies of many companies. Check with your state's insurance department for a list of reputable brokers.

may also be higher or lower depending on where you do business. For example, a salon in Manhattan is likely to pay higher insurance rates than one in the Plains states, where the cost of living is considerably lower.

Determining the level of coverage that best meets your business needs is one of your broker's jobs, but keep in mind that the most important factor in determining that figure is how much risk you're willing and financially able to take. Basically, you want to be sure you have enough coverage to protect yourself against business losses that could close your salon down temporarily or put you out of business permanently. But while insurance protects you and your business from losses incurred by physical damage, negligence, and other factors, not every owner needs every kind of insurance available—not to mention that you probably couldn't afford to insure yourself against every conceivable risk anyway. So instead, work with your broker to figure out which risks you're more likely to encounter in the course of doing business, and then insure yourself adequately against them. Generally speaking, the types of insurance salon owners are most likely to need include liability, malpractice, casualty, workers' compensation, and life/health/disability insurance.

> **Tip...**
>
> ## Smart Tip
>
> A common-sense approach to risk management can help you avoid accidents in the salon. For instance, don't let employees do work they're not qualified to perform; eliminate hazards that can cause someone to trip or fall, including snow and ice in your parking lot; and ensure electrical outlets aren't overloaded.

Liability Insurance

Liability insurance is probably the single most important coverage you'll need for your new business. It protects your business assets against damages and/or lawsuits due to human error for which you can be held liable. It also covers your business against accidents and bodily injuries that can happen on the premises, including everything from slip-and-fall injuries to burns from piping hot coffee served to a waiting customer.

Because claims for such injuries and loss can be devastating to a business, be sure to obtain enough coverage for your salon. Insurance industry experts recommend obtaining $2 to $3 million in liability coverage, which shouldn't break the bank because the price isn't calculated on a dollar-for-dollar basis. Rather, the cost is typically determined by the size of your business (usually in terms of assets, square footage, or number of employees) and the risks involved in day-to-day operations.

Be sure not to skimp on this coverage since the sky's the limit on lawsuit awards these days, and just one legal action could put you out of business permanently. Your insurance broker or salon industry association can guide you about how much coverage to buy, and the cost can vary tremendously depending on where you do business. One caveat about liability insurance policies: They often have a lot of exclusions. Your insurance broker can help you understand exactly what is and isn't covered so you're not caught unprepared in a crisis.

> ## Smart Tip
> **Tip...**
>
> For a quick overview of all the business insurance you may need, as well as other common types of personal insurance, check out the Insurance Information Institute at iii.org and Insure.com at insure.com.

Malpractice Insurance

No, you don't have to practice medicine to need malpractice insurance. This type of insurance, which is also known as errors and omissions insurance, covers you against damages due to negligence, errors, omissions, and wrongful acts that can be attributed to your professional practices, like the bad perm mentioned at the beginning of this chapter. With the increase of baseless lawsuits in this country and the astronomical awards made to plaintiffs who win these sometimes ridiculous legal actions, it makes sense to have malpractice insurance so one day you won't lose everything you've worked for because someone decides she isn't happy with the hairstyle your new employee gave her.

Casualty Insurance

Since you never know when Mother Nature will decide to send a tornado roaring through your community or a curling iron left plugged in overnight will ignite and cause your salon to burn down, you need sufficient casualty insurance to cover your losses. Casualty insurance protects you against major disasters, such as floods, earthquakes, hurricanes, fire, vandalism, and so on. It can be expensive, so work closely with your insurance broker to determine the level of coverage you need and for which contingencies. For example, if your shop is on the San Andreas Fault, then earthquake insurance is a must. But if your shop is in Phoenix, flood insurance probably isn't necessary.

Workers' Compensation

While all the insurance mentioned so far is advisable but not mandatory, you have no choice when it comes to workers' compensation insurance. Every state requires employers to have this insurance, which compensates employees for work-related injuries, diseases, and illnesses. It's "no-fault" insurance, meaning the employer doesn't have to admit responsibility for the injury or illness, and the employee doesn't have to sue to get compensation.

Fun Fact

The Uniform Workmen's Compensation Law, which was enacted to protect workers who are injured on the job, was created in 1910. By 1960, every state had adopted some version of the law. Hawaii was the last state to join the fold in the 1960s.

Unfortunately, workers' compensation insurance is a complicated issue and can't be discussed in depth here. But you can get a handle on what the regulations and rules are for your state by visiting workerscompensationinsurance.com, which has links to government resources for each state.

Despite the fact that each state has its own requirements, there are still universal things you can do to minimize your costs. To begin with, work closely with your accountant to estimate your payroll costs accurately for the first year. If you underestimate your annual payroll, you could receive a hefty audit premium at the end of the year from your state's workers' compensation board. Furthermore, you can reduce costs by minimizing the risk of injury in and around your salon. For example, if you're in a snowy locale, keep your parking lot shoveled and salted during the winter to prevent slip-and-fall accidents. Place anti-slip mats by the front door during wet weather to prevent falls inside your building, and keep your salon tidy (no wet towels on the floor, for instance) for the same reason.

By the way, just in case you're wondering, you personally don't count as an employee under workers' compensation law.

Business Interruption Insurance

This type of insurance replaces income lost due to an event that causes the business to close, like a fire, theft, or other insured loss. It also may cover expenses like equipment replacement, lease or mortgage payments, and so on. The price is determined by how likely you are to face certain risks. For instance, the premium cost could be higher for a salon owner than, say, a sporting goods store owner because of the possibility of fire from the equipment you use (like hair dryers or curling irons) or the flammable liquids in use (like hairspray). Also, because it would be difficult for you to operate out of

Smart Tip

Tip...

In the event of a loss, it's crucial to have good insurance records. Be sure to keep receipts for every item purchased for the salon; keep a written inventory of each item that notes the date of purchase, price, and current value; and either photograph or videotape the contents of each room. Then keep these documents in a safe place (such as a safe deposit box).

Cover Me, I'm Goin' In

As mentioned previously, you can get insurance to guard against just about any kind of risk. Other types to consider include:

○ *Glass breakage insurance.* Replacement insurance for your business's all-important window on the world. After all, it gives passersby a tantalizing glimpse of the great work your stylists are doing—and someday might make a tantalizing target for an out-of-control driver.

○ *Fidelity bonding.* This is so-called "honesty" insurance to protect you against theft by an employee.

○ *Life insurance.* A must for protecting your family or significant other in case of your death, life insurance is sometimes looked at as a prerequisite to obtaining financing from banks.

○ *Disability insurance.* If you can't work due to injury or illness, this type of insurance will replace a percentage of your gross income.

○ *Health insurance.* Though expensive, many salon owners offer health insurance as a benefit to employees because it's such a good recruiting and retention tool. Group rates generally are lower, so it may be more affordable than you think to offer health benefits. In addition, health insurance premium costs are 100 percent deductible for self-employed business owners, so the net impact on your business actually will be zero.

With all these options, it's probably clear that you need to find yourself an experienced insurance broker. To get the process rolling, turn to the Business Insurance Planning Worksheet on page 64 to make notes on the types of insurance you may need.

another location if you were temporarily displaced, the cost could be somewhat higher than a standard policy. Your insurance broker can counsel you on whether to have this insurance and how much it would cost.

Computer Whiz

One last professional you definitely should have on your business team is a computer consultant who makes shop calls. No matter how much you like to tinker with your computer, you're unlikely to have time for that once you're a small-business er. So find someone who not only can handle the mundane tasks like updating your system, adding hardware or software, and optimizing computer performance, but also can design, update, and maintain your website.

If at all possible, ask a friend or business associate for a referral to make sure you get someone who's both experienced and qualified. Computer consultants usually charge by the hour, and you can expect to pay $50 an hour and up for their services.

Business Insurance Planning Worksheet

Type	Required	Annual Cost	Payment Schedule
General liability			
Malpractice			
Casualty			
Workers' compensation			
Life			
Health			
Disability			
Other			
Other			
Other			
Total Annual Cost			$

Home Chic Home

Establishing a Salon/Spa Location

Choosing a location for your salon/spa is another one of those important decisions you'll make in the early stages of establishing your new business. Obviously, you'll want to locate it in an area that's easily accessible by highway or byway, with plenty of traffic (both foot and the four-wheeled variety) and parking. The surrounding area should be attractive, well-lit, and safe. There should also be other retail businesses nearby (as opposed to parks or a regional airport) because they can generate business for you as they attract customers through their own doors.

Typically, salons operate out of three types of establishments: freestanding buildings, storefront properties, and shopping centers like strip malls. Occasionally, salons are located in malls, but it's actually more common for them to operate out of a freestanding building located on the perimeter or an "outlot" of the mall property because the rent is so high inside the mall. They're also sometimes found on the ground floor of office buildings in large metropolitan areas where there's a significant amount of foot traffic during the business day. However, such locations may not be optimal if they're in an urban area that doesn't have much traffic in the evenings or on weekends.

Your choice of location will be driven not only by the amount of startup funding you have but by the size of the facility you want to have, the availability of space in the city where you want to do business, the local competition, and your tolerance for building/renovating and wrestling with local zoning requirements.

Building Basics

Free-standing buildings are the choice of many salon owners because of their high visibility in the community. Buying such a facility, whether it's a two-story Victorian home-turned-business with fanciful curlicues on the outside and gorgeous wood floors inside, or a space previously occupied by another business, can be a good choice because you'll have more latitude when it comes to renovating and decorating. You control the fixed costs like overhead, utilities, and (within reason) the terms of the mortgage. You also don't have to pay common-area charges, like for snow removal, advertising costs, and security that are incurred when you're in a strip mall. Finally, you'll have the tax advantages of owning the building.

If you have the time and great organizational skills (not to mention nerves of steel), you might consider building your dream salon. That, of course, requires hiring an architect, dealing with the local zoning commission, contracting with and overseeing the work of a builder and his/her contractors and subcontractors, and myriad other details. It can be done,

> **Tip...**
>
> **Smart Tip**
> When signing a lease, look for clauses that can benefit a startup business, like a bail-out clause, which allows you to get out of the lease if your sales don't reach a predetermined amount, or a co-tenancy clause, which lets you break the lease if the anchor store in the shopping center or mall closes or moves out.

but you might be wiser to start out in an existing building instead since you can have your business up and running a lot faster and with fewer headaches.

Leasing a free-standing building gives you some of the same advantages as buying, although you'll have a landlord to deal with. But you usually can negotiate favorable terms upfront, so leasing is certainly a viable option.

Debbie Elliott of Debbie Elliot Salon & Day Spa in Portland, Maine, made a lot of sacrifices early in her career as a salon owner so she could afford to lease a building

---

The Lease You Can Do

Like a residential lease, a commercial lease is an ironclad contract. No matter what happens to your business, you'll be contractually liable for the entire amount of the lease. For that reason, try to negotiate a lease with the shortest term possible—say, for one or two years. That gives you a safety net in case you outgrow your shop sooner than expected or you decide you'd prefer another location.

When negotiating, always ask for an option to renew for five years at a predetermined cost. The option to renew is important—it prevents you from losing your lease at the end of the lease term and having to re-establish your business at a new location before you're ready to go.

Some types of commercial leases you might encounter include:

○ *Gross lease.* You pay only rent, while the landlord shells out for the taxes, insurance, and other property costs.

○ *Net lease.* Besides rent, you'll pay a portion of the maintenance fees, insurance costs, and other expenses.

○ *Triple-net lease.* The renter pays for everything. This type of lease is common with freestanding buildings.

○ *Shopping center lease.* The renter pays a base rent amount tied to the square footage of the space, as well as a percentage of shopping center overhead costs like advertising, maintenance, and property taxes. Typically this type of lease also requires the tenant to pay a percentage of gross monthly sales to the owner. That might sound distasteful, but if the center is in a prime location, it might be worth the financial sacrifice.

○ *Step lease.* With this type of lease, the rent goes up annually to cover the cost of inflation. Tax and insurance premium increases are usually part of the deal.

of her own. Admittedly, it wasn't much of a building; she says it really should have been condemned. But she opened a 250-square-foot salon on the ground floor of a 1912 facility and lived upstairs to save money. "The ceiling in the bedroom was so low that I could [lie on the bed and] put my foot on the ceiling and paint my toenails," Elliott says with a laugh. "The kitchen was also too tiny for a table, so I used the top of my piano as a breakfast bar."

One reason for Elliott's meager start was that she wasn't able to get financing for her first salon. She believes the odds were stacked against her from the beginning because the perception is that the salon industry is notorious

Dollar Stretcher

Be ready to negotiate the lease prepared by your landlord. It's not set in stone (or legally binding) until you sign on the dotted line. If you realize later that there's a condition you don't agree with, you have no recourse but to grit your teeth and keep mailing those monthly checks until the lease expires.

for underreporting income, including tip income. As a result, she started the business with less than $10,000 and the help of her boyfriend—who later became her husband—and friends who helped out for free until she was able to hire them. "I really am the poster person for no financing," Elliott says.

Another owner who leased and then invested big bucks in renovations is Pat Millar of Clinton, New Jersey–based Millar Salon Spa Store. When she was ready to expand into spa services, she leased a former dry cleaning building (one of only two available locations in her small town) and then spent $150,000 to renovate everything—from the floors to the walls to the ceiling—and buy furniture and skin-care equipment.

If you don't want the responsibility of a free-standing building, you should consider leasing space in a shopping center or a strip mall. These are choice locations because of the exposure they offer. They're usually anchored by a large or well-known retailer, such as a drug store or grocery store, which serves as the gravitational force that pulls traffic in for all the other establishments in its orbit. Lest you be concerned that you could one day be ringed by bigger and fancier salons, take heart. Leasing agreements usually have provisions that limit the number of similar businesses that can roost in the same shopping center or strip mall, as Angela Marke found out when she and partner Andrew Bernard leased space for a salon in a strip mall in Macomb, Michigan. BoRics (a hair-care franchise) was already a tenant in the shopping center when she opened, but because Marke's salon provides cutting, styling, and finishing rather than providing the express services the franchise chains are famous for, the salons weren't considered to be in competition by the management leasing company. And the proximity of the other business, which eventually moved out, never hurt her business because Andrew Marke's clientele is 90 percent working women and young mothers. Unlike BoRics, the salon handles very few children.

One common complaint from strip mall tenants is that hefty marketing and maintenance fees are built into the leases. So inquire about them carefully before you sign on the dotted line so you don't get an unpleasant surprise after you've paid all your bills out of your net receipts.

Sometimes an opportunity comes along that's too good to pass up, as Dennis Gullo discovered when he opened his first salon, Moments, in 1978. "I happened to see an ad in the local paper for a salon in a shopping center," says the Mount Laurel, New Jersey, salon and spa owner. "It had only been open for six

Smart Tip

Good parking is almost as important as the building in which you house your salon. If your building doesn't have sufficient, well-lit parking, consider leasing additional space from a nearby business. Or if there's a parking structure nearby, validate clients' parking tickets. The small cost will be worth the goodwill it will generate.

months. I looked at the equipment and the décor and paid what it would have cost me to build. It was an expedient way to get into business, and the salon was beautiful. It was finely appointed and in fact was even nicer than my home!"

Storefront properties are also popular, particularly in communities with historical or renovated downtown areas. Like a strip mall, these facilities are part of a string of stores with common walls on either side. The difference is that strip malls can spring up anywhere, including in residential areas, while storefront properties generally are part of a business district that stretches for blocks or even miles. If you can find a storefront property to lease in a bustling downtown area, grab it immediately. If it's in a resort town with year-round activities, use yourself as a human shield to bar other potential business owners from entering the building until you can put your John Hancock on the lease papers. That's how good that kind of property can be.

Good as New

There's one other type of property that deserves serious consideration when you're looking for a place to set up shop. A facility that once served as a hair salon may be a good choice for your new location. The good news is, a lot of the infrastructure you'll need, including extra plumbing, special electrical outlets, and maybe even fixtures like salon stations and the reception desk, may already be onsite and available for purchase with the building. The bad news is, there might be a good reason why the salon closed, like there's too much competition in the area, the location is crummy, or the previous owner had a poor reputation among clients and in the community. The same goes for a salon that's currently in business but is up for sale.

If you're seriously interested in taking over an existing or now-defunct shop, you need to find out exactly why the shop is on the block. Also, check the shop's financial records for the previous three years to look for trends like declining sales. If it's still open, observe the shop's activities for a few days, noting daily volume and clientele. Also, determine the worth of any equipment or fixtures left behind and decide whether you'll actually be able to use them. Finally, consider remodeling costs vs. the expense of starting with a blank slate in a different facility.

> **Bright Idea**
>
> Since working on a concrete floor (even one that has tile over it) can be hard on the feet of stylists who must stand for up to eight hours at a time, install a wood or vinyl floor covering in the cutting area. Add anti-fatigue mats behind each chair to further reduce foot fatigue.

To find an existing shop for sale, check the advertising section of your local newspaper and shopping center publications, or contact a real estate broker or rental agent. Some of the salon industry publications (a few of which are listed in the Appendix) also have classified sections where salons may be advertised for sale.

Shop Talk

All this talk about finding a building to buy or lease is fine, but unless the space is the right size, it won't matter how much you love that quaint storefront in a seaside village or the art-deco-themed strip mall in the suburbs.

Salons usually range from 1,200 to 2,000 square feet, although small spaces can be considerably smaller (fewer than 1,000 square feet)—this does not include your spa area, which we'll discuss in detail in Chapter 8.

You'll need four separate areas in your hair salon: reception and retail, shampoo, cutting/service, and storage. The largest of these, of course, should be your salon services area, which should take up about 50 percent of the floor space. About 20 percent of the space should be allotted to retail/reception, 10 percent to the shampoo area, and the remaining 20 percent to storage and an employee break/lunch room area. The employee/client restroom and your office also should be located in this area. If space permits, you may want to provide a one-person changing room for customers who are having treatments like color or perms. Otherwise, the restroom can serve as a changing room. Be sure to put a large hamper in the changing room/bathroom for collecting soiled smocks. A final necessity for salons is a closet or cloakroom, which should be placed in front of the salon, either in or next to the reception area. It should have doors (bifold doors will suffice) to keep the area looking tidy.

The reception area should be tastefully decorated and brightly lit, with an attractive reception desk and one or two stools for employees and comfortable seating for five to 10 clients (the more stations you have, the more chairs you'll need in the reception area). Space permitting, a coffee table where you can display hairstyling books and magazines is a nice touch. Use a small corner of the reception area for a coffeemaker or coffee service, a complimentary amenity that will be much appreciated by clients and staff alike. (Of course you'll have to designate someone to keep an eye on coffee levels and make a new pot when the brew runs low.) In keeping with the principles of feng shui, the Chinese art of placement for harmony, you might want to use plants as a natural divider to separate the reception area from the spa, but low walls are also acceptable. The idea is to define the two spaces but allow clients to dally over coffee and see into the salon while they wait.

Smart Tip

Chemical treatments like color should be applied at the back of the salon, preferably near the shampoo bowls and away from the reception area. This keeps strong chemical smells from permeating through the salon and protects the ego of your valued customers, who might not want to be seen with foil or hair color in their hair.

Your retail products also should be displayed in this area, possibly on a handsome glass and metal baker's-style rack or on shelves attached to the wall. This display should be placed near the cash register for easy access and upselling by the person working the register. You may wish to display additional retail products on glass shelves behind the reception desk, but you may find it looks more stylish if you hang artwork or perhaps a wall fountain behind the desk instead.

The shampoo area is usually located toward the back of the salon and is equipped with shampoo sinks (either free-standing or affixed to the wall) and chairs. Each station should also have a "back bar," or cabinet, for storing products used in the salon, like shampoos, conditioners, and deep-conditioning treatments. Naturally, these should be the same products you sell in the retail area, and your stylists should be trained to discuss each product used with the client as a way to spur sales.

Each stylist station requires about 125 to 150 square feet, according to Spa Equipment International, a division of Salon Equipment International in Bellflower, California, and consists of a hydraulic chair and a cabinet or credenza for storing equipment. Each countertop should have wells for storing a blow dryer and curling irons. An average-size salon will have four to six stations on each side of the room, for a total of eight to 12 chairs.

If you plan to offer nail services, you'll need to carve out a space near the front of the salon to accommodate a manicure station. One way to fit the station into the salon area easily is to eliminate one or two stylist stations, depending on how much room you need.

▲

The break room should be located toward the rear of the salon and take up no more than 5 to 10 percent of the total area. For example, in a 1,000-square-foot salon, the break room would be no more than 10 by 10 square feet. Equip it with a table and chairs, a sink, and a microwave oven, and/or small refrigerator so your employees can chill out between clients rather than sitting in a stylist's chair (which doesn't look professional and gives clients the impression that the shop isn't very busy). It also provides an alternative to leaving the salon in search of a cold drink or something to eat. Consider placing the break room near the back door to the salon so anyone who smokes can step outside for a smoke break rather than traversing the length of the salon and huddling outside your front door.

Of the remaining floor space, about half should be allotted for a storage room, which can be used to house basic cleaning supplies and retail product overstock. Have sturdy shelves installed along one wall so products can be organized and rotated easily. The other half should be designated as office space so you have somewhere to conduct performance evaluations, meet with vendors and work on your computer without interruption. The most you'll probably be able to squeeze into an office in a 1,000-square-foot salon is a small desk with a computer and a chair, a visitor's chair, and perhaps a file cabinet or a small bookcase. To ensure that serious work can be done here, have adequate lighting installed. Recessed lighting is especially nice in a small work area because standard ceiling fixtures can cut into the space and make it look even smaller.

You'll probably need to employ an architect to design a salon that uses all the space optimally. John Palmieri of Scizzors in Shrewsbury, Massachusetts, did just that even though he already had a good idea of what he wanted in his salon. He enlisted the aid of an architect friend who used a computer to design a virtual salon, and was even able to see how the salon would look under various lighting conditions at various times of the day, thanks to the wizardry of computer software. But if you have the confidence to go it alone, you could use a draftsperson instead to draw a design you can show to your builder. You can find a draftsperson in the Yellow Pages under Drafting Services.

One final option is to work with a hair salon/spa equipment company to design your space. Some companies, including the Beecher Group (iowabeauty.com), offer complimentary design services, obviously as a loss leader to get you to buy your equipment from them. In fact, you can go to Beecher's website at iowabeauty.com/html/salon_layouts.html right now to see five floor plans to use an idea starter.

Getting the Look

Today's hair salons are trendy, chic, and even entertaining places. Some have lighted cutting platforms (some of which revolve) where a master stylist can showcase his or her talents for the benefit of the people in the reception area. Others have gimmicks like lights that flash in synchronization to pulsing music as it pounds through an elaborate sound system. But the one thing they all should have is style. After all, people go to hair salons because they want to look great, so your salon décor should reinforce the idea that this is a place where magic happens.

Start by tailoring the salon's décor to reflect the tastes of the clientele you want to attract. Are you after youthful, free-spirited trendsetters? Then flashy colors, edgy art, and funky chrome fixtures are for you. Want the monied crowd? Then a traditional color scheme with lots of dark wood, tasteful wallpaper, and armoire-style stations might be appropriate.

Use color strategically throughout the salon. Certain colors, like blues and greens, are calming and soothing, and tend to make an area look larger. On the other hand, reds and yellows have great energy and would be good to use (although probably not together) in the main salon and reception areas, where you want the mood to be upbeat and dynamic.

Another trick you can use to make compact areas seem larger is to place mirrors in strategic places. Add spotlights or track lighting if you want to make certain areas, including your retail area, seem more prominent.

Your floor covering is an integral part of the décor, too. While the cutting and shampoo areas need a durable floor covering that can be cleaned easily, it doesn't have to be boring. Vinyl floor coverings are now available in wonderful patterns ranging from hardwood to faux marble. You might prefer to install carpeting in the reception area, but keep in mind that a darker color might be a better choice since carpeting can become quickly soiled in inclement weather.

Tell Them About It

One last thing you'll need to generate buzz for the biz is appropriate signage for the front of your building. Signs create an image for the salon, they show your existing customers the way to the front door, and entice passersby to stop in. For that reason, they should give the name of the salon in bold letters, followed by a brief description of the services you offer if the salon name doesn't adequately describe them. For instance, a salon called Chez Cheri should have "Hair and Nail Designs" in smaller letters under the name, or the public might think the place is a French bistro.

In addition to exterior signs, which typically are illuminated from within, you might consider neon or other well-lit signs for the windows that advertise certain services (like "creative color" or "European manicures"). Just be sure they don't block the view into your salon, since that's one of your best ways to attract new business.

Signage is fairly costly but truly is worth the price. Check with the local zoning commission before you invest big bucks in your signs. You wouldn't want to be standing outside admiring your expensive new sign and have the city fathers careen into your parking lot and cite you for violating a city ordinance concerning size or design. This is particularly true in communities with historic preservation districts where it's a practically a capital offense to alter so much as a brick in the facade of a historic landmark.

Respect for tradition and workmanship was the driving force in Debbie Elliott's decision to work with the many original features found in her first salon, which was built in 1912. "The building told us what to do, just like hair tells you what to do," says the owner of Debbie Elliott Salon & Day Spa. "There was a lot of stained glass in the building and a lot of other things that were of good quality, but they were covered up when someone made bad decorating choices in the '60s and '70s. We spent six months ripping out stuff that shouldn't be there, and we filled four commercial dumpsters."

While many of the points discussed in this chapter also apply to spas, you'll find a more in-depth discussion of spa design and décor in Chapter 8.

The Cutting Edge

Hair Salon Equipment

Now that we've discussed some of the more pedestrian aspects of getting your new salon up and running, it's time to talk about all the equipment you'll need to start your business and provide salon services. If you've been a hairstylist for a while, you're already well aware of the many tools you need to practice your profession. In this chapter, you'll of those supplies, as well as information about the furniture and other

e equipment you need before you can usher your first client through

of this chapter, you'll find three useful information sheets, each fol-

rksheet, that will help you to determine which supplies and equipment are necessary for your startup, as well as their costs. The charts on pages 92, 94, and 99 refer to two hypothetical salons (Chez Cheri on the low end and Jamie Lynn Hair Designs and Day Spa on the high end). The worksheets on pages 93, 97, and 100 may be used to note your own startup expenses, salon equipment and supplies, and office equipment expenses. Spa equipment is touched on in the salon equipment worksheet, but Chapter 8 deals with it in detail.

Personal Pampering Paraphernalia

While some stylists prefer to use their own cutting and styling tools, it's not uncommon for a salon owner to provide everything his or her employees need to do their job. The items typically found at a stylist's station include:

- Blow dryer
- Diffuser
- Scissors
- Electric razor
- Trimmer
- Combs (wide-toothed, rake, rattail, regular)
- Disinfectant jar
- Small and large round brushes
- Vent brush
- Paddle brush
- Sectioning clips
- Plastic control clips
- Curling iron
- Flat iron
- Velcro rollers in various sizes
- Hot rollers
- Plastic processing caps
- Cutting capes

Bright Idea

According to *NAILS* magazine, the best ways to interest salon customers in nail services, include making sure your stylists have their nails done in the shop, offering complimentary hand massages to waiting customers so you can talk up your services, and putting pictures of people getting their nails done on the wall above the shampoo bowls and on the mirror of every stylist station.

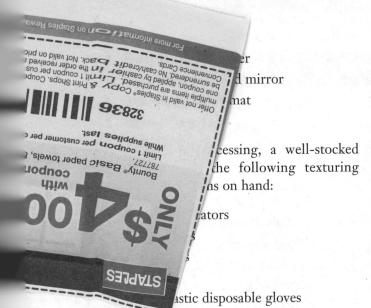

... er ... mirror
... mat

... cessing, a well-stocked ... the following texturing ... ns on hand:

... ators

- ... astic disposable gloves
- Mixing bowls
- Plastic protective capes
- Texturizing (perm) rods/rollers
- Timer
- Tint applicators
- Highlighting caps
- Mixing whisk
- Processing, neutralizing caps
- Stylist aprons
- Weave caps

In addition, to keep the styling area tidy, you should have at least a couple of push brooms and dustpans near the stylists' stations, as well as several trash cans strategically placed near the back work room or the rear entrance. You'll also need a good supply of towels stored near the shampoo bowls, preferably out of sight in a shampoo bulkhead.

You'll find a checklist of the typical salon products you'll need, including styling and color products, on page 78.

Nail Tools

If you plan to offer nail services in your salon, you'll need the following basic supplies for each manicurist station: nail polish, nail polish remover, nail clippers, nail files and buffers, cuticle pushers, cuticle scissors, orange sticks, and finger bowls. A more comprehensive manicure and pedicure supply checklist is found on page 79.

Salon Product Checklist

Styling Products

- ❏ Color care shampoo, conditioner
- ❏ Conditioner (normal, dry, color-treated)
- ❏ Curl crème, amplifier
- ❏ Curly hair styling gel
- ❏ Deep conditioner
- ❏ Dread shampoo, conditioner, wax, tightening gel, removal shampoo
- ❏ Dry shampoo
- ❏ Gel
- ❏ Hair finishing spray
- ❏ Hair fixative
- ❏ Hair glue, hair cement
- ❏ Hair serum
- ❏ Humectant pomade
- ❏ Leave-in conditioner
- ❏ Modeling clay, paste
- ❏ Mousse
- ❏ Pomade
- ❏ Root lifter
- ❏ Shampoo (normal, dry, color-treated)
- ❏ Shine spray
- ❏ Styling spray
- ❏ Styling wax
- ❏ Thickener
- ❏ Volumizer

Color/Processing Products

- ❏ Beard and mustache color
- ❏ Bleaching products
- ❏ Developer
- ❏ Gray hair color products
- ❏ Hair color correction
- ❏ Hair color protection
- ❏ Henna
- ❏ Highlights
- ❏ Lowlights
- ❏ Permanent color
- ❏ Peroxide
- ❏ Relaxer
- ❏ Semi-permanent color
- ❏ Straightener
- ❏ Temporary hair color
- ❏ Texturing (perm)

Fixtures, Salon Furniture, and Hardware

Now on to the equipment you'll need to serve customers, work on the books, display your retail products, and store all the supplies you'll be using. You'll find that when it comes to buying salon fixtures and furniture, the process is a little like buying a car. You'll want to check out all the options and comparison shop to find what you like best at a price that fits into your budget. And while you can't take a new shampoo

Manicure and Pedicure Supply Checklist

Your manicurist is the professional who will require the most equipment and supplies to do his or her job. The good news is that many of these supplies are bought only occasionally and in large quantities, so you can do a lot of manicures and pedicures with what you have on hand.

Here's a checklist of the various supplies (other than capital equipment like manicurist tables, which are discussed in this chapter) your manicurist/pedicurist will need:

Manicures

- ❏ acrylic nails
- ❏ acrylic nippers
- ❏ adhesive
- ❏ alcohol
- ❏ antiseptics
- ❏ application brushes
- ❏ assorted artificial nails
- ❏ base coats
- ❏ cotton
- ❏ cuticle oils and creams
- ❏ cuticle pushers
- ❏ cuticle scissors or nippers
- ❏ emery boards
- ❏ finger bowls
- ❏ hand creams and lotions
- ❏ heaters for oil
- ❏ measuring spoons
- ❏ mending silk
- ❏ mixing bowls
- ❏ nail bleaches and whiteners
- ❏ nail cleansers
- ❏ nail clippers
- ❏ nail dryers
- ❏ nail files and buffers
- ❏ nail forms
- ❏ nail glue and resins
- ❏ nail hardeners
- ❏ nail polish
- ❏ nail polish remover
- ❏ orange sticks
- ❏ sculpted nails
- ❏ small application brushes and spatulas
- ❏ thinners
- ❏ tissues
- ❏ top coats
- ❏ towels
- ❏ tweezers
- ❏ ultraviolet light (for curing acrylic resins)
- ❏ wet sanitizers

Pedicures

Same items as for manicures, plus:

- ❏ acetone
- ❏ antibacterial soap
- ❏ astringents
- ❏ toenail clippers
- ❏ water basin/foot bath
- ❏ white block buffer

Tip...

Smart Tip

You can buy with confidence if you purchase salon equipment and other items from online auction sites. Services such as eBay have internal safeguards as well as fraud protection and dispute resolution services to make sure buyers are satisfied.

bowl for a test drive, you may be able to visit a salon equipment showroom near you to see the stuff in person. One of the largest suppliers is Salon Equipment International (SEI), which has a massive showroom in Los Angeles (and was the source of the sample prices in this chapter). You'll find its address, along with contact information for several other large suppliers, in the Appendix.

If you can't make a personal visit to a showroom, try calling one of the suppliers and asking if any of the salons in your area have the equipment you're interested in. Then stop by the salon to see it up close and personal. But don't make a clandestine visit. Do the owner the courtesy of informing him or her about your mission. It's likely the owner won't mind if you take a look around.

If you're on a tight budget, consider buying used equipment and fixtures from professional equipment dealers or salons that have gone out of business. You could save as much as 50 percent off the price of the same equipment when new. To find used equipment, check the Yellow Pages under Beauty Salons–Equipment & Supplies–Wholesale as well as the classified section of your closest big-city newspaper.

Debbie Elliott in Portland, Maine, was able to save a lot of money when renovating her modest first salon by using salvaged materials. For instance, she bought scrap marble for $3 a square foot and mirrors for $29.95 each from a salvage company. When cleaned up and installed, it was impossible to tell the difference between the scrap materials and new. She also bought mahogany flooring for $1 a square yard that was left over from a commercial job. Another prized find was a $20 chandelier that she literally took off a garbage truck, then refurbished and beautified. "I had to put the business together very creatively in the beginning," she says.

Another great potential source of used equipment is online auction sites. A recent check of eBay yielded numerous listings for salon equipment, including one for a complete four-station salon package. It included four styling chairs, two shampoo units, two dryer chairs, and four rolling carts, all for $3,250. Shipping was free. Other auctions offered a new

Dollar Stretcher

If you're looking for used equipment, be sure to check out Craigslist.org, which allows you to search the geographical areas of your choice to find bargains on used merchandise. The geographical search feature is important because you'll rarely or never find Craigslisters who are willing to ship merchandise to you.

glass top, contemporary reception desk for $850 (plus $148 shipping and handling), and new rolling carts with tray tops for $73 each (plus $24 shipping). If you watch carefully, you might be able to find used equipment at much lower prices. The downside to buying on eBay is that some of sellers won't ship at any price, so it's up to you to make arrangements to pick up the items yourself. So read auction listings carefully before you bid.

Reception/Retail Area Equipment

You know the old saying: First impressions are lasting impressions. That makes your reception area one of the most important parts of your salon since it's the place your clients see first. You'll want to choose furnishings that are stylish yet comfortable, in colors that accent your salon's overall décor.

You'll need enough seating for six to ten people in the reception area of an average-sized salon. While individual chairs are much more attractive, many salon owners choose one-piece banks of seats in groups of three or four that can be placed against the walls. Individual chairs sell for around $200 each, while banks of three chairs are around $780. Suppliers like SEI also sell reception couches, which are plushly upholstered and have padded armrests in between each seat; they run about $300. If space permits, add end tables or coffee tables on which you can display styling books and perhaps a fresh flower arrangement. You also should have a magazine rack to hold more styling books and magazines, as well as a complimentary coffee service on an attractive stand.

The reception desk is such a focal point that you should budget as much as possible for its purchase. There's such a wide assortment of desks, from art deco to high-tech metal, in shapes from straight as an arrow to U-shaped, that it's impossible to discuss them all here. The main criterion (besides cost) is that the desk fits the image you want for your salon. You can pick up a basic wood model for about $1,100, while a high-style version can run much more. (For example, SEI's stunning Eurisko reception desk, with stainless sides and an illuminated front panel, runs $5,100.) Of course you'll also need one or two task chairs (possibly on casters and preferably with a back since they're more comfortable) to use behind the desk. Budget about $300 each for these.

Smart Tip

Tip...

The type of music you play in the salon should reflect the tastes of your clientele, not of the stylists or other employees. If you're shampooing and perming in a retirement community in Florida, you shouldn't be playing rap at ear-splitting decibels. "Soft rock" or "elevator muzak" are usually pretty safe choices for most salons.

Naturally, you'll also need a multi-line telephone for the reception desk, but we'll talk about phones in the office equipment section later in this chapter.

One piece of equipment that bears mentioning now is your cash register, which will occupy a place of honor on your reception desk. There are a couple of ways to cache your cash. The first is to buy an electronic cash register. A basic model like the Sharp ER-A320 retails for about $289. A helpful add-on is a laser barcode scanner, which starts at about $150 and can be used if you plan to sell gift cards. You'll also need a

Smart Tip

If you decide to offer complimentary beverages to clients waiting for services, be sure to include flavored coffees and herbal teas on the refreshment table or cart. In particular, teas like peppermint and chamomile are refreshing and will put clients into a "spa" frame of mind.

receipt printer that kicks out those little slips of paper that are signed when customers make a credit card purchase. The Epson TM-U200D impact printer runs $290. You can find local dealers who sell this type of equipment in the Yellow Pages under Cash Registers and Supplies, as well as online by Googling the name of any of the equipment discussed here.

If space is an issue or you don't want to mar the elegant lines of your reception desk with a cash register, you'll want to use a point-of-sale (POS) cash drawer instead. Cash drawers are receipt printer-driven, and can be attached via a USB, serial, or parallel port. A cash drawer starts at around $150, but be sure it will work with your printer before you buy. A lot of companies, including Salon Iris (saloniris.com), offer packages that include all the POS equipment you'll need. The Salon Iris package is discussed later in this chapter.

If you're planning to sell retail hair-care products such as shampoo, conditioner, mousse, and wax (and you really should), you'll need either a display case or a shelving unit to showcase your wares. Unless the configuration of your reception area is unusual and you need custom-built displays, you can order standard display cases from salon equipment companies. A cube-style display case with adjustable shelves costs around $775 while a six-foot wall display unit goes for around $2,450. Wall shelves can be an attractive alternative and can be either painted or stained to match salon décor. Glass shelves will give the salon a more contemporary look.

You should consider buying used display fixtures if you're on a budget. Check your newspaper's classified section for retail business liquidations as a starting point. Used display fixtures should cost about 50 percent less than new ones.

The salon's sound system should be located in the reception area and controlled from the reception desk. Expect to pay up to $2,000 for a commercial sound system with installation. You might also consider placing a TV in the salon area as a distraction for clients waiting for color to process or as an out for people who don't wish to chat with their stylist. You can pick up a 37-inch flat panel TV for as little as $599 at an electronics store like Best Buy.

Finally, don't forget to include artwork if there's wall space. Another decorator option is a wall fountain, which is a natural choice for a spa because water therapy is considered soothing. While it's impossible to put a price on artwork like paintings or prints, a 30-by-36-by-7.5-inch wall-mounted glass waterfall fountain is about $775 from a company like Soothing Walls (soothingwalls.com).

Salon Equipment

As with the reception area, you can buy fixtures and furniture in a wide range of prices. Each stylist station should include a large mirror that's hung at least at the height of most stylists (which is 5 foot 10 inches for the average-size American man), counter space for equipment, and storage cabinets, drawers or bins for brushes, combs, clips, and other tools. Select stations with wells for a hair dryer and curling irons, as well as an outlet strip. If you're short on space, you might choose an upright free-standing "rollabout" styling station, and then mount a large mirror on the wall, facing the styling chair.

A budget-priced styling station like the QSE Styling Station from SEI starts at around $675. A 36-by-42-inch mirror starts at around $270. A basic wall-mounted styling station with a mirror like the Heritage Styling Station from SEI starts at about $500. Naturally, you can spend far more for the really deluxe models, like a Eurisko styling station to match the reception desk mentioned earlier, which can run $2,000 or more. A free-standing Formica rollabout station starts at about $280, while a handsome wood styling cabinet is around $800.

You'll also need hydraulic chairs to raise and lower the client to a level that's comfortable for the stylist to work. An all-purpose styling chair in vinyl (both adult- and kid-sized) starts at around $400. A half-round anti-fatigue mat starts at around $70; a rectangular mat is about $90.

Hand-y Work

Although you'll need a lot of supplies to stock your manicurist station, you don't need too much equipment. The main expenditure will be for a manicurist table, which comes in regular and space-saving models. Like stylist stations, you can spend a lot of money on the table depending on the finish; a basic model with a work light starts at around $300. A ventilated table, which collects dust and fumes and channels them through a filtering system, increases the price to well over $1,000. You'll also need a stool or a manicurist chair (starting at around $125).

Pedicure equipment includes a pedi spa chair and matching technician stool. The moderately-priced Maiden Spa Pedicure System from SEI is $3,200, although you can spend far more. For instance, the Murano pedicure spa system starts at $11,350. A more basic unit with a heated footbath massager runs about $400.

It's also strongly suggested that you invest in an autoclave that can be used for any of the personal care implements discussed in this chapter, including scissors, and manicure and pedicure implements. An autoclave uses steam to sterilize personal care tools and prevent cross infection. At about $1,000, the cost may seem high, but having an autoclave in your salon sends a message to your clients that you care about good health and cleanliness. A sanitizer also will do the job and costs just $200.

Bright Idea

Hot rock hand massage is a popular manicure add-on. After a nongreasy lotion is applied by the manicurist, small river rocks (which are heated in a crockpot) are placed in the client's palms. Smaller stones are placed between the fingers, and then a warm towel is wrapped around each hand. The treatment both relaxes hand muscles and relieves stress.

Shampoo Station Equipment

Your basic equipment will include sinks (either wall-mounted or pedestal) or "backwash" units that include the shampoo bowl and chair, and possibly a cabinet known as a bulkhead or back bar with a countertop for storing supplies. The faucets and waterspout are usually sold separately.

You'll need about one bowl for every three stylists. According to SEI, you'd have to use your kitchen sink for 70 years to equal the wear your salon shampoo bowls will get in just one year, so buy the best you can afford. Wall-mounted shampoo bowls start at around $250, while a backwash unit starts at around $850. A shampoo bulkhead with storage for salon products and towels starts at about $1,200.

A basic shampoo chair starts at around $100, while a deeply padded, deluxe model like the electric Futura Shampoo Chair that reclines and has a padded kickout leg rest starts at about $1,100.

Floor hood dryers start at $215, while dryer chairs are $200 and up. Additional equipment you may wish to purchase upfront includes a hair steamer ($459 and up), a hair processor (around $1,000), and an infrared heat lamp (about $1,300).

Keep in mind that when you're purchasing salon equipment, you might be able to negotiate a better price by asking for package pricing. Don't write any checks or hand over your credit card until you investigate every discount option available.

And by the way, unless your new salon space was previously occupied by a hair salon (or perhaps a restaurant), you should expect to have additional plumbing installed in the shampoo area. It's possible you'll also need plumbing and a 220-volt electric line or gas line for the washer and dryer you'll use to launder towels and smocks.

Employee Lounge and Workroom Equipment

Here are a couple of areas where you can definitely buy used if the budget demands it. Furnish the lounge with a used table and chair set found at a secondhand dealer, a yard sale, or through the classifieds. You might also add a microwave oven and a small refrigerator so your employees don't have to run out for lunch or soft drinks.

Since your workroom will be used for everything from storing towels and retail products to mixing tints and dyes and washing towels and smocks, go for basic shelving and storage cabinets (like the type you can buy at home improvement stores), which are both practical and durable.

Unless you want to drag the soiled towels and aprons home with you every night and fluff and fold all night, you should invest in a washer and dryer for the salon. While heavy duty models are preferred, basic models should be adequate when you start out. A basic Kenmore washing machine runs about $330 at Sears, while a dryer is about $400; and they're often on sale.

Security Equipment

No matter where you set up shop these days, the potential for break-ins and vandalism exists. Head off trouble by having a security system installed in your new salon. A closed-circuit video surveillance system, POS monitoring system, and building alarm all may be necessary to safeguard your business and assets.

For the purposes of this book, we're assuming that the building you'll be buying or leasing will already have a security system. But if you do need to install more or upgrade the existing equipment, you have a number of options. A local alarm isn't connected directly to a central alarm company monitoring station or police department, but it's loud and can attract unwanted attention that will scare off mischief-makers. Silent alarms are connected to a monitoring station, which notifies the police when the alarm is tripped. Perimeter or entry alarms sound if someone tries to enter your shop, while space protection alarms use infrared beams or motion detectors to determine whether someone is in your facility illegally. It's a good idea to select a system that has battery or other emergency backup in case of a power failure.

Depending on where your shop is located (say, in an urban area or an isolated location), you may need a combination of alarm types to protect your shop adequately. Companies like ADT, Brinks, and Guardian all install commercial alarm systems, or you can consult the Security Control Equipment and Systems category in the Yellow Pages for leads to other security system vendors and installers. It's also possible that the same company that installs your sound system will be able to install your security equipment, so be sure to ask because you might be able to get packaging (read: discount) pricing.

Office Equipment and Supplies

Now that your salon is fully outfitted (at least on paper), let's focus on the items needed behind the scenes to keep the salon humming along. Among them will be office furniture, computer and other office equipment, and office supplies.

Furniture

Chances are that when you design the layout of your new salon, one of the areas that will be allotted the least amount of space will be your office. But it's an important space because it will be used for everything from conducting employee reviews to scrutinizing invoices. Your office is also a little oasis of quiet and solitude and, like the spartan quarters of cloistered nuns, needs to have only the basics to be functional.

Since your customers will never see your office, it's OK to furnish it with an inexpensive or secondhand desk or computer workstation. You'll also need a comfortable office chair (preferably one that's ergonomic to minimize back discomfort), and a sturdy two- or four-drawer file cabinet.

If you go new, check out office supply stores like Staples or Office Depot, which sell reasonably priced desks for $50 to $250, and chairs for $50 to $200. Ready-to-assemble furniture is also affordable, as is used furniture, which you can find through newspaper classified ads or Craigslist. A two-drawer letter-sized file cabinet costs as little as $40, although a higher-priced model may be the better buy because its drawers extend fully, making it easier to remove file folders from the very back.

Beware!

Make sure the door to your salon office can be locked securely. In addition to keeping confidential employee records secure, a lock will keep your laptop or desktop computer from disappearing when the salon is busy. Only you and your salon manager should have a key to the door.

Personal Computer

You can get a lot of computer for the money these days. For example, one deal we spotted was for the Dell Inspiron 530s with a 320GB hard drive, DVD-RW drive, and a 17-inch widescreen flat-screen monitor for just $549. A basic laser printer runs as little as $150 at an electronics store like Best Buy.

If you prefer to tote your computer along with you wherever you go, then a laptop might be a better choice. The HP Pavillion laptop was just $749 at Best Buy at the time this book was written, and there were a number of other snappy models priced under $1,000. Add in a wireless printer like the HP Officejet 6000 for $119 and you'll be good to go.

If you have a little more money to spend, other useful add-ons include a scanner (which ranges from $100 to $150) and a Zip drive ($100 to $150) for long-term storage.

Software

Most of the salon owners interviewed for this book use two basic software packages for conducting business: Microsoft Office and QuickBooks Pro. Microsoft Office Professional includes Word, Excel, PowerPoint (which would be useful for creating shop training materials), Access (for database management), Publisher (which has newsletter templates), Accounting Express, and Outlook e-mail. Office retails for $499.95, or $329.95 for the upgrade. QuickBooks is an easy-to-use accounting package that keeps your financial records straight, manages your business checking account and prints checks. QuickBooks Pro retails for $199.95 (although it's possible to find it discounted for less at places like Amazon.com).

There are dozens of specialty salon and day spa management software packages on the market that can be used to manage the many details involved with operating a salon, writing a business plan, and handling online appointment scheduling. Google "salon software" or "spa software" to find others you can explore.

- *Salon Iris software (saloniris.com)*. Geared toward hair salons and spas, Salon Iris Software has powerful POS functions like appointment scheduling, client and inventory tracking, and online booking compatibility. Other useful features include general ledger, tip tracking, mailing list creation, profit and loss statements, and a time clock, to name just a few. The software is compatible with most cash drawers and barcode scanners. You can connect two computers with the network package, which costs $1,899. The professional version (which doesn't include networking) costs $1,199. You can purchase a professional package that includes Iris Professional, a cash drawer, a thermal receipt printer, and a bar code scanner for $2,099. Add in a keyboard with an integrated credit card scanner and credit card processing software and setup, and

▲

you'll pay $2,499. The manufacturer, CMJ Designs, offers a fully functional trial copy that can be used as long as you like with no obligation to buy. It also offers a payment plan.

- *Unique Salon Software (salonpages.com).* This software, which bills itself as the most complete and user-friendly salon software available, really does have an extensive list of features, including POS functions, unlimited client recording and tracking, payroll and tax functions, inventory tracking and automatic retail percentage markup, booth rental functions, unlimited booking, accounts payable and general ledger functions, gift card programs, marketing tools, and much more. The entry-level product is $395; the top product (Unique Pro Software with Hardware) is $1,695 and includes the software and POS hardware.

- *Leprechaun Spa & Salon Software (leprechaun-software.com).* With everything from a client database with unlimited entries, POS register compatibility, and appointment scheduling to salon/spa marketing tools, this software package was designed by salon owners specifically for salon management. Rather than paying upfront for the software, then paying for updates and service, you subscribe for $59 a month. You can request a free demo CD to try it yourself.

- *QuickPlan Salon and Day Spa (quickplan.com).* This low-cost software package is just $195 and is used specifically to help you write a salon and day spa business plan. It includes templates for the business description, industry analysis, marketing strategy, financial plan, and a five-year forecast. It also includes employee and operations manuals, and SBA forms to make it easier to apply for loans. You receive a hard copy of the plan, a CD-ROM, and immediate download access.

- *Millennium (harms-software.com).* A product of Harms Software, Millennium is actually a small-business management tool rather than a salon/spa–specific package. But it's still considered one of the industry's leading software choices. It has an advanced appointment book, inventory management and employee applications, gift card and marketing tools, and more. The affordable small-business version for a three-computer network costs $1,995.

Fax Machines

A fax machine is convenient for sending orders to suppliers or requesting information. A standard plain-paper model costs about $100 (although Office Max recently offered a $60 rebate on an HP standard fax machine, bringing the cost down to $40). A multifunction machine that also scans, copies, and prints starts at as little as $300. If you decide to install your fax machine on a dedicated telephone line, the installation fee will run $40 to $60, plus you'll incur the cost of the monthly phone service.

Telephones and Answering Machines

Make sure you buy the best model you can afford since you and your staff will be using the phone constantly. A standard two-line speakerphone with auto-redial, memory dial, flashing lights, mute button, and other useful features runs $40 to $150, while a top-of-the-line business phone can cost $250 or more.

A stand-alone answering machine costs $15 to $65, while a high-quality cordless phone/answering machine combo will run $99 to nearly $200. Buy the best you can afford so it will serve you well. You may find that voice mail is a better choice for your salon.

Bright Idea

When recording your voice-mail or answering-machine message, play the same kind of music in the background that you play in your salon so it becomes your salon signature. Of course, keep the decibel level down so callers can actually hear the message.

Cell Phone, BlackBerry, iPhone

If you're one of the four people left on the planet who doesn't have a cell phone, you definitely should get one now that you're a small-business owner—and that goes double for you if you'll have employees. If you need a phone, start by investigating the plans that provide a free phone with service activation. One such company is Verizon, which at press time had a $59.99 monthly plan that included a free Samsung Gleam phone and a Plantronics Explorer 232 Bluetooth headset when you sign a two-year contract.

Of course, if you want "cool," then you'll need a full-featured phone like a BlackBerry or iPhone instead. These devices give you internet access, instant messaging (IM), and text messaging capabilities, and in the case of an iPhone, literally thousands of apps (iPhone-speak for "application") to help you do everything from downloading music and setting your DirecTV DVR from afar to watch Queen Latifah in *Beauty Shop*, to fighting space invaders and fitting a mini Pilates workout into your busy schedule.

In the corporate world, iPhone (iphone.com) is actually considered more of a multimedia entertainment device than a business tool, but hey—you're entitled to a little fun, especially if you left the corporate world behind when you started your salon. iPhone reviewers say that its apps are much more advanced and nimble than BlackBerry's, but the device's QWERTY keyboard isn't as user-friendly. A 3G iPhone starts at $199.

A BlackBerry smartphone (blackberry.com) is a combination e-mail, Bluetooth-enabled cell phone, wireless internet, IM, and GPS device. As with an iPhone, additional apps, including organizational tools and games, can be purchased right from your phone. The BlackBerry Pearl starts as low as $99, while a high-end RIM BlackBerry Bold is more than $659.

Copy Machine

Having a copy machine in your office is a real convenience, though not a necessity. But since they're really reasonable—priced at as little as $250 for a desktop machine to $2,000 or more for a standard business machine—it might be worth the money. Toner cartridges are readily available from your local office supply store start at around $125.

Office Supplies

A salon won't be a big consumer of office supplies, but you'll still need the standard stuff, like Post-Its, pads, file folders, pens. Your office supply budget also should cover the cost of your business cards, brochures, and service menus (a brochure-sized document that has the prices of all the services you offer). A quick print shop like FedEx Office or an online printing company such as ColorPrintingCentral.com can design and produce all these items for you. To get the most competitive quote, use an online source like Print Quote USA (printquote usa.com). All you do is type in the specs for your job, and the site will do the rest. A casual price survey revealed that 1,000 full-color 8½x11-inch brochures printed on good quality paper run around $185, while 1,000 color business cards are $50. Office supply stores like Staples and Office Depot also offer affordable printing services, and you can place your order online and pick it up in the store. A 1,000-count box of standard one-color business cards runs about $30.

Excluding the cost of your business cards and direct mail materials, about $20 a month on average should cover anything you need. Allot about $50 if you'll need copier paper, too.

Go for It

If you've been filling in numbers on the worksheets in this chapter, you can now tally up all the estimated costs to get a pretty clear idea of how much capital it will take to get your new salon up and running. (The only expenses still missing are your spa costs; those are covered in Chapter 8.) If it looks like you're going to need some financial help to make all this happen, check out Chapter 14 for advice about approaching bankers and obtaining financing.

If you'd like to see a sample of typical expenses before you fill out your worksheet, refer to the charts on page 99 that shows equipment costs for two hypothetical salon/day spas. The smaller shop, Chez Cheri, is a sole proprietorship with four stations and one full- and two part-time employees. Jamie Lynn Hair Designs and Day Spa is a C corporation and has 10 stations and five full- and two part-time employees on the salon side. The business also has a full-time aesthetician. Both salon owners are full-time employees and work behind the chair.

Chez Cheri is located in a leased 800-square-foot space in a strip mall, while Jamie Lynn Hair Designs and Day Spa is in a 2,000-square-foot building purchased by the owner. Owner Jamie Lynn purchased top-of-the-line equipment and furniture for her facility to promote her image as an upscale salon. She also offers full spa services, including hydro treatments. Chez Cheri purchased good-quality used and lower-end equipment to save money and offers manicures, facials, and waxing as an entré into the spa business.

You'll notice that prices aren't filled in for every item on the charts. We've made some assumptions about what are most appropriate and likely purchases for a startup salon/day spa. But we've included the line items anyway in case you decide you want to purchase them when you launch your business.

Startup Expenses

Item	Chez Cheri	Jamie Lynn Hair Designs and Day Spa
Rent (security deposit and first 6 months)	$7,200	
Mortgage (six months)		$15,600
Leasehold improvements	$8,000	$15,000
Exterior sign (lighted, 30 x 96-inch)	$1,000	$1,000
Salon/spa equipment and supplies (capital expenses)	$20,971	$126,919
Initial retail inventory	$1,000	$2,750
Office equipment, furniture, supplies	$3,920	$6,015
Business license	$15	$15
Phone (installation of 2 lines)	$80	$80
Utility deposits	$150	$150
Employee wages and benefits (first 6 months)	$30,000	$94,050
Taxes (first 6 months)	$5,400	$12,660
Startup advertising	$400	$2,000
Legal services (incorporation)	$500	$500
Insurance (total annual cost)	$600	$1,200
Market research	$250	$1,000
Professional association membership dues	$90	$410
Publications (annual subscriptions, professional and consumer for reception area)	$22	$100
Internet service (broadband; first 6 months)	$480	$480
Website design	$2,000	$2,000
Web hosting, domain name	$60	$120
Subtotal	$82,138	$282,049
Miscellaneous expenses (roughly 10% of total)	$8,200	$28,200
Total	**$90,338**	**$310,249**

Startup Expenses Worksheet

Item	
Rent (security deposit and first 6 months)	$
Mortgage (first 6 months)	
Leasehold improvements	
Exterior sign	
Salon and spa equipment and supplies (capital expenses)	
Initial retail inventory	
Office equipment, furniture, supplies	
Business license	
Phone (installation of 2 lines)	
Utility deposits	
Employee wages and benefits (first 6 months)	
Taxes (first six months)	
Startup advertising	
Legal services (incorporation)	
Insurance (total annual cost)	
Market research	
Professional association membership dues	
Publications (annual subscriptions, professional and consumer for reception area)	
Internet service (Broadband; first 6 months)	
Website design	
Web hosting, domain name	
Subtotal	
Miscellaneous expenses (roughly 10% of total)	
Total	$

Salon Equipment/Supplies

Salon Furniture/Equipment	Chez Cheri (4 stations)	Jamie Lynn Hair Designs and Day Spa (10 stations)
Budget station with mirror	$2,000	
Deluxe station		$20,000
Mirrors (24-by-36-inch)		$2,700
Rollabout cart	$840	
Hydraulic chairs	$1,600	$4,000
Anti-fatigue mats	$360	$900
Shampoo bowls	$500	
Shampoo chairs	$200	
Backwash		$2,550
Shampoo bulkhead		$3,600
Dryer (floor)	$430	$1,075
Dryer chair	$400	$1,000
Hair processor	$1,000	$1,000
Hair steamer	$459	$459
Infrared heat lamp	$1,300	$1,300
Professional blow dryers	$200	$2,000
Professional ceramic curling irons	$200	$2,000
Professional flat irons	$240	$600
Misc. professional hair care/styling products (est.)	$1,000	$2,000
Manicure table, light	$300	$2,000
Mani technician stool	$125	$250
Pedicure cart	$400	
Pedi spa chair		$3,200
Misc. mani/pedi supplies (est.)	$300	$600
Autoclave		$1,000
Instrument sanitizer	$200	
Reception desk	$1,100	$5,100
Task chair	$300	$600

Salon Equipment/Supplies, continued

Salon Furniture/Equipment	Chez Cheri (4 stations)	Jamie Lynn Hair Designs and Day Spa (10 stations)
Reception desk computer	$1,000	$2,000
Salon productivity software package with cash drawer, receipt printer, barcode scanner		$1,899
Salon productivity software alone	$395	
Decorative waterfall		$775
Mouse pad	$10	$20
Surge protector	$20	$40
Cash register		$289
Cash register rolls (carton)		$25
Cash drawer	$150	
Receipt printer	$290	
Barcode scanner	$150	
Reception area chairs	$600	$1,560
37-inch flat screen TV	$600	$600
TV Mounting bracket	$50	$50
Workroom, Employee Lounge, Misc.		
Table, chairs	$100	$300
Microwave	$80	$80
Refrigerator	$100	$200
Workroom shelving	$100	$200
Workroom cabinets	$100	$200
Sound system	$1,000	$2,000
Washer, dryer	$730	$730
Retail Products and Supplies	$1,000	$2,000
Product display unit	$775	$2,450
10-by-13-inch paper retail product bags (1,000)	$40	
Imprinted white Kraft paper gift bags (500)		$550
Two-line price label gun	$120	$120

Salon Equipment/Supplies, continued

Workroom, Employee Lounge, Misc.	Chez Cheri (4 stations)	Jamie Lynn Hair Designs and Day Spa (10 stations)
Price labels (1 box)	$37	$37
Spa Equipment and Supplies		
Hydraulic facial chair		$900
Illuminated magnifying lamp		$150
Facial trolley		$350
Facial technician stool		$100
Vacuum/spray machine		$600
Rotary brush machine		$300
Steamer		$400
Hot towel cabinet		$140
Epilator		$2,000
Wax warmer	$70	
Paraffin masque bar		$495
Massage table		$6,200
Massage technician stool		$100
Essential oil diffuser		$75
Hydrotherapy tub		$24,000
Scotch hose		$4,800
Swiss shower		$7,500
Vichy shower		$3,000
Jacuzzi/whirlpool tub		
Steam cabinet		
Miscellaneous spa supplies		$1,000
Miscellaneous retail spa products		$750
Total expenses	**$20,971**	**$126,919**

Salon Equipment/Supplies Worksheet

Salon Furniture/Equipment	
Budget station with mirror	
Deluxe station	
Mirrors (24-by-36-inch)	
Rollabout cart	
Hydraulic chairs	
Anti-fatigue mats	
Shampoo bowls	
Shampoo chairs	
Backwash	
Shampoo bulkhead	
Dryer (floor)	
Dryer chair	
Hair processor	
Hair steamer	
Infrared heat lamp	
Professional blow dryers	
Professional ceramic curling irons	
Professional flat irons	
Misc. professional hair care/styling products (est.)	
Manicure table, light	
Mani technician stool	
Pedicure cart	
Pedi spa chair	
Misc. mani/pedi supplies (est.)	
Autoclave	
Instrument sanitizer	
Reception desk	
Task chair	
Reception desk computer	
Salon productivity software package with cash drawer, receipt printer, barcode scanner	
Salon productivity software alone	
Decorative waterfall	
Mouse pad	
Surge protector	
Cash register	
Cash register rolls (carton)	
Cash drawer	
Receipt printer	
Barcode scanner	
Reception area chairs	

Salon Equipment/Supplies Worksheet, continued

Salon Furniture/Equipment	
37-inch flat screen TV	
TV Mounting bracket	
Workroom, Employee Lounge, Misc.	
Table, chairs	
Microwave	
Refrigerator	
Workroom shelving	
Workroom cabinets	
Sound system	
Washer, dryer	
Retail Products and Supplies	
Product display unit	
10-by-13-inch paper retail product bags (1,000)	
Imprinted white Kraft paper gift bags (500)	
Two-line price label gun	
Price labels (1 box)	
Spa Equipment and Supplies	
Hydraulic facial chair	
Illuminated magnifying lamp	
Facial trolley	
Facial technician stool	
Vacuum/spray machine	
Rotary brush machine	
Steamer	
Hot towel cabinet	
Epilator	
Wax warmer	
Paraffin masque bar	
Massage table	
Massage technician stool	
Essential oil diffuser	
Hydrotherapy tub	
Scotch hose	
Swiss shower	
Vichy shower	
Jacuzzi/whirlpool tub	
Steam cabinet	
Miscellaneous spa supplies	
Miscellaneous retail spa products	
Total expenses	$

Office Equipment/Supplies

Office Equipment	Chez Cheri	Jamie Lynn Hair Designs and Day Spa
Computer, printer	$1,000	$1,000
Software		
Salon software		$2,000
Microsoft Office	$500	$500
QuickBooks	$200	$200
Surge protector	$20	$20
Fax machine	$100	$100
Copy machine	$250	$1,000
Phone	$70	$500
iPhone/BlackBerry	$200	$200
Answering machine	$15	$65
Security system	$700	$1,200
Office Furniture		
Desk	$100	$100
Chair	$50	$200
File cabinet(s)	$40	$80
Bookcase(s)		$100
Office Supplies		
Business cards, letterhead, envelopes	$200	$200
Salon service menus	$185	$185
Miscellaneous supplies	$50	$50
Computer/copier paper	$25	$50
Extra printer cartridges	$25	$75
Extra fax cartridges	$55	$55
Extra copier toner	$125	$125
Mouse pad	$10	$10
Total	**$3,920**	**$8,015**

Office Equipment/Supplies Worksheet

Office Equipment	
Computer, printer	
Software	
Computer, printer	$
Software	
Salon software	
Microsoft Office	
QuickBooks	
Surge protector	
Fax machine	
Copy machine	
Phone	
iPhone/BlackBerry	
Answering machine	
Security system	
Office Furniture	
Desk	
Chair	
File cabinet(s)	
Bookcase(s)	
Office Supplies	
Business cards, letterhead, envelopes	
Salon service menus	
Miscellaneous supplies	
Computer/copier paper	
Extra printer cartridges	
Extra fax cartridges	
Extra copier toner	
Mouse pad	
Total	$

The Serene Scene

Spa Equipment

Up to this point, we've spoken in general terms about spas as part of a hair salon. But the moment of truth has arrived. Now that you've started to make decisions about the type of facility you want to buy or lease, you also must decide whether you want to include a day spa in your plans.

▲

Spas have become so popular in the past decade that many hair salons now offer some type of spa services, such as massages and facials, as a way to capitalize on the trend. You can easily do the same thing in your new hair salon without going to the trouble and expense of establishing a true day spa. You simply designate a room in your salon for these body-care services, equip it properly, hire the appropriate personnel, and start advertising your spa services.

According to industry experts, a true spa offers water therapy in addition to skin-care services, even if it's only a shower/massage service. So if you're determined to operate a day spa along with your salon, you must be prepared to make a substantial investment in capital equipment and supplies upfront, as well as invest in a larger building since a spa often requires a significant amount of space. For example, it's not uncommon for high-end, stand-alone luxury spas to be as large as 4,000 square feet, although you can design a lovely, upscale facility in as little as 1,000 square feet. An architect can help you determine exactly how much room you'll need.

In this chapter, we'll discuss today's typical spa customer, and then explore in detail the types of services offered in a true day spa, the special licensing that may be required by your state, and the general equipment needed to operate a first-class spa.

A Booming Market

While technically everyone, from kids to senior citizens, is a prospective spa client because everyone can benefit from good·skin care, baby boomers are most likely to be your best customers. Not only are there a lot of them—75.8 million Americans were born in the Boomer years—but they're also a generation on a mission to retain or regain their youth. They grew up hearing about the dangers of spending too much time in the sun without sunscreen and the benefits of eating five to seven fruits and vegetables daily for good health. They are interested in anything that relieves stress while providing the feeling of well-being that comes from looking their best. So they're primed for services like those found at a spa because such services can help improve their appearance and/or preserve their health.

This is not to say you should overlook other prospects like senior citizens, who definitely can benefit from the improved skin texture and tone afforded by body-care services, or teens, who may be interested in acne treatments for the face and back, and specialty services like facials (especially before important social events like homecoming or the prom). And certainly, many other women from 20 to 46 will be interested in electrolysis, massage, facial treatments, and so on. But you'll want to pay special attention to those folks born between 1946 to 1964, who tend to have both the money and the inclination to take good care of themselves.

The Spa Experience

As mentioned in Chapter 2, services such as manicures, hair removal, and makeup application are all part of the spa experience, but there are four specific skin- and body-care services that are the hallmarks of a true spa: facials and body exfoliation, massage, wraps and packs, and hydrotherapy.

Saving Face

Facials are often the first service a new spa client will try. While women constitute the majority of facial clients, men are having facials in increasing numbers, partly for their perceived anti-aging benefits. Mud, seaweed, and aromatherapy masks are often used to achieve a healthy glow.

The equipment needed to offer facials includes a hydraulic facial chair that can double as a waxing chair, which starts at about $900; an illuminated magnifying lamp with a stand ($150 and up); a stainless-steel facial trolley for holding implements ($350); and a stool for the cosmetologist (about $100). Other specialized equipment includes a vacuum/spray machine for stimulating circulation, eliminating product residue, and loosening blackheads ($600); a rotary brush machine for sloughing off

Like a Rolling Stone

Hot stone therapy has been rocking the spa industry for several years now, but the technique is actually centuries old. It has been used for everything from pain relief to promoting the health of the body, mind, and spirit, and spas incorporate stones in treatments such as reiki and reflexology, as well as shiatsu and deep-tissue massage, manicures and pedicures, and even facials.

When used with massage, stone therapy is actually a type of acupressure. Placing the stones on certain parts of the body is said to encourage better energy flow, or chi, throughout the body. Some aestheticians also use cool gemstones as part of a deluxe facial to soothe and tone the skin. Gemstones also are often placed on the seven chakra points during treatments. Chakras are considered the main energy centers of the body in Eastern medicine, and applying certain gemstones to the chakras can heal and soothe. For example, placing rose quartz on the heart chakra is said to improve the interaction of all the other chakras, which include the root, sex, stomach, throat, brow, and crown chakras.

dead skin cells and removing impurities ($300); a steamer ($400); and a hot towel cabinet ($140). Some equipment companies like Spa Equipment International (SEI), which was the source for many of the prices in this chapter, offer multifunction skin-care units with attachments that run about $2,500. Note that all the prices given here are opening price points for reliable equipment. You definitely can spend a lot more depending on the brand and features of the items you choose.

Finally, you'll need supplies like cotton, spray bottles, gowns, cleansers, toners, and masks.

A licensed cosmetologist may give facials without additional licensing. Usually his or her salon training will include basic facial techniques, but some additional training may be needed to learn how to use the specialty skin-care equipment properly.

Body exfoliation is an extension of facial care and usually involves the use of masks, salts, and polishes to give skin a natural, healthy glow by removing dead skin. Some popular treatments include salt glows, which are mineral salts from sources like the Dead Sea mixed with lotion or oil and spread over the body. Enzyme peels are smooth substances, often from fruit sources, that dissolve dead skin, while body polish contains abrasive ingredients, such as nuts or ground pumice that are mixed in a creamy base and remove dead skin and polish the body. Body masks are used to soften and smooth the skin; popular masks include mud and warmed paraffin. Seaweed is also a popular spa treatment because of its high mineral content, which is thought to improve metabolism.

Smoothing the Way

Speaking of exfoliation, depilation (hair removal) is one of the most sought-after spa services, right behind facials. Spas usually do a big business in both permanent (electrolysis) and temporary hair removal (waxing and threading).

A diode laser system (epilator) is used for permanent hair removal. Some systems can also be used for general dermatology procedures, including age spot removal, wrinkle reduction, laser resurfacing, tattoo removal, and more. A basic diode laser system starts at $2,000, while a system that can handle dermatology procedures starts at about $4,500. Only a licensed electrologist should use this equipment for depilation, even though many manufacturers will sell the equipment to anyone who has the cash to buy it. It also should be noted that in some states, including Connecticut, laser hair removal can only be performed by a physician, physician's

Bright Idea
Other revenue-generating services you may want to offer at your spa include skin resurfacing and dermabrasion, glycolic and chemical peels, teeth whitening, tanning (both sunless and with a tanning bed), lash and brow tinting, seated facials with makeup application or application lesson, and holistic energy work like Reiki, reflexology, and guided imagery.

assistant, or a nurse under the direction of a physician. Be sure to check with your state cosmetology board to find out what's allowed.

For temporary waxing, you'll need a wax warmer, which on the low end can be as little as $70, or $495 for a multi-compartment paraffin masque bar.

Hands-On Appeal

Perhaps the second most popular spa treatment is therapeutic massage. There are several types of massages, including Swedish, shiatsu, manual lymph drainage, and deep-tissue massage.

> **Bright Idea**
>
> If you have enough room, create a "relaxation room" in the spa where clients can relax after a service and let their cares drift away. Keep the room softly lighted, provide comfortable furnishings and play soothing music so clients can put their feet up and close their eyes for a few peaceful moments.

The basic equipment needed for massage services includes a padded massage table ($400 for a standard table that can double as a facial table, up to $6,200 or more for a deluxe table like the Sonora Sound Table, which has a built-in Bose sound system, electronic controls, deluxe wood construction, and more). You'll also need a chair or stool for the massage therapist ($100), and supplies like treatment gowns, towels, cotton, massage oil and creams, and spatulas. Add an essential oil diffuser for $75 and some lovely scented oils to make the massage experience even more pleasant.

Most states require special training and licensing for massage therapists. Check with your state cosmetology board to find out about requirements.

All Wrapped Up

Body wraps and packs are used to reduce the appearance of cellulite, cleanse the body of impurities, and reduce water retention. These treatments are popular with women because they produce a temporary slimming effect and leave them feeling refreshed. Basically, such treatments consist of applying a mud, algae, or other compound to the skin, and then wrapping the body to intensify the healing action of the product.

Popular wraps include herbal wraps, which are linen sheets that have been soaked in an herbal concoction, and then wrapped comfortably around the body and covered with rubber sheets to keep the wrapping warm for around 30 minutes. Seaweed wraps are usually made of plastic or Mylar foil and are useful as a cellulite treatment. Spot wraps are also used for cellulite, for treating sore muscles or areas like the lower back, and for increasing circulation. Compounds with healing properties like mud and algae products may be used under the wraps.

The same equipment used for facials and massage, including the facial chair or massage table and the electrical equipment used for facials, can be used for wraps. In addition, you'll need plastic wrap, elastic bandages, linen wraps, foil, and the natural compounds used on the skin. Cleansing creams and other treatment creams are also commonly used.

No licensing beyond a current cosmetologist license is required to provide wrap and pack therapy.

Under the Sea

What's believed to be the most beneficial of all spa treatments is also the most costly to provide. Hydrotherapy treatments are used to cleanse and balance body functions like circulation, and may use seawater (a process called thalassotherapy) or fresh water (balenotherapy). Hydrotherapy equipment includes:

> **Bright Idea**
>
> The latest trend in spa décor is using "green" materials. Cork floors, which are softer to walk on than wood as well as less expensive, are popular, as are fountains that rain down on green plants to simulate a rain forest. Bubbling water walls are another way to evoke the soothing sensory nature experience.

- *Hydrotherapy tub.* This is a tub with strategically placed water and air jets that massage various parts of the body. An air wand also can be used by the technician for underwater treatments like back massage. A hydrotherapy tub is a huge expenditure at $24,000 to $36,000. The high-end models include fiber-optic colored lights and electronic self-disinfecting systems.

- *Scotch hose.* A high-pressure jet hose used by the technician to spray water at various parts of the body provides deep tissue and muscle massage, and stimulates circulation and eliminates toxins. It's usually used with the Swiss shower (described next). The spray is so strong that the client actually has to hold on to handles built into the wall of the shower to stay balanced. This equipment runs about $4,800.

- *Swiss shower.* This $7,500 piece of equipment has multiple hydrojets for high pressure lymphatic and cellulite treatments or showerheads that direct warm and cold water toward certain parts of the body as a way to improve circulation.

- *Vichy shower.* With its multiple heads that dispense fine sprays of water or pressurized jets of water, the Vichy shower is used to relax sore muscles and to relieve stress. It's also used to rinse mud, seaweed, salt glow, and other treatment packs from the body. Unlike the Swiss shower, which is used standing up, this equipment rains water down on the reclining client. A wet table with Vichy shower is about $3,000, while a wall-mounted unit is about $4,800 (the wet treatment table is extra).

Combination hydrotherapy units are available, and save both money and space. One such unit from SEI is a combination hydrotherapy tub, wet table, steam capsule, and Vichy shower—and will put you back $36,000. An economy model, which doesn't include the tub, runs $18,000.

Other types of hydrotherapy equipment commonly found in a spa include a sauna, Jacuzzi/whirlpool tub, and steam cabinet. The latter is used with essential oils to rid the body of toxins, help clear the sinuses, and improve breathing. The moist heat also is recommended for spas in warmer or more arid climates, where a sauna might be too drying, according to Colleen Blevins-Lunsford, former owner of Wolf Mountain Day Spa in Grass Valley, California, who now resides in England.

Getting the Look

As you can see, setting up a spa involves a large cash investment and enough room to incorporate all the wonderful toys you'll use to make people look beautiful and feel great. Assuming you have both, let's address spa design issues next.

The overall spa layout should be created by a professional designer or an architect. That's because unlike a hair salon, which tends to be a large open area with few partitions or walls, a spa needs to be somewhat compartmentalized. However, if you've worked in or visited enough spas in the course of your career, or you have good visualization skills, you may already have a good idea of how you want your spa to look. In that case, it may be possible to work with a draftsperson to draw up plans for the spa, and then hire someone to build the space for you. You can find a draftsperson in the Yellow Pages under Drafting Services.

Spas are usually divided into a series of rooms that are used as changing and showering facilities, treatment rooms, consultation rooms (for discussing treatment options and post-treatment care), and so on. The consultation room may also be used as an office when not in use by an aesthetician and a client, although we'll assume you'll have your main office in the salon area. There should also be a retail area that's separate from the hair salon's retail area (so customers aren't confused or distracted by products that don't relate to spa treatments). The spa and the salon can share a reception area, however, as long as it's centrally located and easily accessible to both sides of the business. Ideally, the reception area will be in the center, with the salon and the spa radiating to either side. If possible, incorporate a supply room in your spa area. If that's not possible, spa products can share storage space with salon products, but strive to keep them separate and organized for easy accessibility.

Bright Idea

Another way to extend your reach and bring in new spa customers (if you have the room to do it) is to offer health club–style "vitality" services, such as yoga, tai chi, and Pilates. These services can be marketed as body therapies for people who want to feel younger, while emphasizing that massage and skincare services make them look younger.

To maximize privacy and make clients feel more comfortable, design the spa so they can go directly from a changing room to a treatment room without having to pass through the spa's more public areas. A small, discreet sign placed on the wall just outside the treatment room door that indicates the room is in use is also a good idea.

> ## Smart Tip
> Use moisture-resistant epoxy grout in wet rooms rather than water-based grout, which collects mildew and will be more difficult to keep clean.

Separate treatment rooms are needed for wet and dry services. While good overhead lighting is needed in treatment rooms both before and after services are rendered, it should be softly diffused. During procedures like massage and hydrotherapy, the overhead lights should be turned off, and an alternate, softer light source should be turned on to create an atmosphere of relaxation and peace. Adequate ventilation is also a must, as is hot and cold running water so aestheticians can mix dry products or dampen towels during treatment without leaving the room. Finally, the treatment room should have its own sound system, on which relaxing music or nature's sounds should be played. No rap or heavy metal!

The décor in the spa should be in harmony with that of the hair salon in terms of color and style. Generally, colors should be soothing and muted. For example, a color such as orange is too jarring when you're trying to create an atmosphere of calm and serenity, not to mention the fact that your choices of furniture and artwork to complement such a hue would be very limited. If you're color- or design-challenged, consider hiring an interior decorator—preferably one with salon or spa design experience—to help you set the right tone with your décor and furnishings.

You could also hire an artist to help, as Shannon Jenkins did when she was ready to add a spa to HairXtreme, the salon she owns with her husband, Daryl, in Chester, Virginia. She had a vision of how she wanted the spa to look, and as manager Daryl put it, the artist was able to translate those thoughts and create a spa that looked as it did in her imagination.

But if you have a knack for decorating (as well as the time to devote to the project), there's no reason why you can't tackle the job yourself. Colleen Blevins-Lunsford started with literally nothing but four walls and nearly 11-foot-high ceilings in her spa. Then, with the help of her now ex-husband, who happens to be a talented woodworker, she created a soothing retreat enhanced by bone-white walls, art, and architectural details such as decorative columns. She kept the look fresh and interesting for her regular clients by repainting, installing new window coverings, and changing the artwork on a regular basis, and found that the changes were invigorating for her staff, as well.

Speaking of staff, the next chapter covers the personnel you'll need to deliver all the spa services discussed here, as well as the stylists and other professionals you'll need to provide salon services.

The Coiffure Crew

Personnel

One of the more challenging aspects of being a salon owner will be hiring and retaining good employees. This can seem like a daunting task, not just because both of these responsibilities can be very time-consuming but also because there's so much riding on employees' skills. After all, your employees will be the front-line representatives of the business you've lovingly and painstakingly cobbled out of little more than a few loans, some ingenuity, and a lot of "shear" determination. Their ability and talent, as well as their attitudes and work ethic, will influence every aspect of the business, from client retention rate to the bottom line.

While supervising your employees and assessing their performance will be your main job as personnel manager, you'll also be called

Stat Fact

During hard economic times, high-end salons may feel the pinch, but budget salons see business pick up. After all, people still need to get their hair done and will figure out a way to do it inexpensively.

on to be a tax expert and a payroll administrator, a mediator, and a referee. If your salon is small, you'll probably also be a confidante and a friend. That's a lot of hats to wear in one day. But that's the reality of salon management, and it underscores the need to choose your employees very carefully.

As if these internal issues weren't enough, the whole issue of hiring is further complicated by one sticky little problem: There's a lot of competition out there for qualified salon personnel. It's not uncommon for salon owners to camp out on the front steps of the local beauty/barber schools so they can lure as-yet-untried, but talented, graduates to positions behind their chairs. It's also common for rival salon owners to try to lure away talented stylists from each other with promises of more money and better working conditions. Then there's the issue of walk-outs. That's when salon staff—usually stylists—decide they can do better on their own and leave a salon en masse to start their own businesses. Not only does the original salon lose its qualified staff, but it also then must compete for new staff members with the turncoats who left.

But as they say, into every life a little rain must fall. The trick is to weather the storm of adversity and conflict so a little shower doesn't turn into a monsoon. In the meantime, here's a rundown of the salon and spa employees you're likely to need for the day-to-day functioning of your new business, along with some typical salary ranges (which may vary depending on which part of the country you're in).

Owner/Operator

You're an employee, too, so you're first on the list. Your day-to-day responsibilities will include overseeing operations, ensuring customer service is a top priority, making financial decisions, checking salon product and retail product inventory, handling personnel matters, hiring new staff, and assessing employee performance. All this is in addition to providing salon services if you're a licensed, practicing cosmetologist.

If you're not a practicing cosmetologist, it's possible to be an absentee owner. But you'll probably want to be in the salon every day anyway, if only to keep an eye on things and make sure everything is running smoothly. If you're providing salon services as well, you can expect to spend up to 60 hours a week or more in the salon, depending on your bookings.

So how much can you expect to earn for all this hard work? As it happens, there's little (free) data available to indicate what salon/day spa owners earn. However, the latest Job Demand in the Cosmetology Industry survey by the National Accrediting Commission of Cosmetology Arts and Sciences, pegged the average total income for a barber/salon in a full-service salon (excluding tips) at just under $40,000 per year. A barber/salon in a specialized salon earns an average salary of just under $43,000, according to the same survey. On the other hand, a survey conducted several years ago indicated that 2 percent of respondents had earned $150,000 to $200,000 in a recent year.

You're likely to be somewhere in the first group, although some owners prefer to take the lowest possible salary necessary to make ends meet at home and plow the rest back into the business. For example, when he started his shop in 1984, John Palmieri of Scizzors in Shrewsbury, Massachusetts, took whatever was left over after paying the bills. Debbie Elliott of Portland, Maine, was equally frugal. "I used to take a minimal salary so I could focus on the business," Elliott says. "My expenses were low because I lived above the salon, and I didn't need much. I preferred to sacrifice and invest in the company."

Her sacrifices were not in vain. After a few years, the salon had revenues of just under $1 million and employed 12 people, and Elliott now pays herself a very good salary with bonuses.

Salon Manager

While it may be tempting to try to undertake all the management tasks of the new salon yourself rather than hiring a salon manager, try to resist the urge. Unless your salon is extremely small, the price you'll pay for a manager's salary is worth it.

The manager can handle myriad tasks like paperwork, recordkeeping, employee scheduling, and purchasing. He or she will also oversee salon maintenance and handle facility management issues (having a bulb replaced when the sign goes dark, dealing with the landlord if something major needs to be fixed, etc.). This person should have the authority to act on your behalf in your absence. PayScale.com says that the median salary in the United States for a hair salon and spa manager with less than a year of experience is $32,834, while a manager with five to nine years of experience earns a median salary of $35,873.

At HairXtreme in Chester, Virginia, owner Shannon Jenkins takes a salary from the business, but her husband, Daryl, who manages the salon as vice president of operations, takes far less. "My salary is a pittance; it's actually hysterically funny," he says. "It's not the lowest salary in the salon, but it's close to the bottom because I don't perform technical services. Shannon and I do this because we have our eye on the prize—our long-term success."

Hairstylist/Cosmetologist

Your stylists are at the heart of your salon staff. Every state requires stylists to be licensed cosmetologists, so you'll want to check their credentials when they apply for a job. A cosmetology license typically allows the holder to cut and color hair and give manicures and facials. Ordinarily, additional licensing is necessary for services such as massage therapy, but it's possible your cosmetologist will be permitted to give hand and foot massages without extra licenses. Check with your state's board of cosmetology to see what the requirements are.

Hairstylists usually are paid in one of two ways: on straight commission or on a salary basis. Commission-based stylists usually earn 35 to 50 percent for each service they provide (although Angela Marke pays up to 60 percent). Salary-based compensation is becoming more common and is actually easier to calculate since wages are typically paid on an hourly basis. The BLS says the median salary for hairdressers, hair stylists, and cosmetologists, all of whom are lumped into a single statistical category, is $23,140, or $12.82 per hour.

"I was commission-based most of my life," says Dennis Gullo of Hair One in Mount Laurel, New Jersey. "Then I went to Neil Ducoff's Strategies Incubator in 2001, and it changed me. The team-based pay concept he teaches gives you more control and eliminates the 'I'm working for myself' mentality that commission-based pay breeds."

"The biggest mistake an owner can make is not looking at a comprehensive pay system that rewards the type of behavior you want to see in employees, which is team behavior," says Neil Ducoff, founder of Salon Business Strategies in Centerbrook, Connecticut. "If you have a 50 percent independent contractor mentality, you'll never have a unified team vision, and that's what helps grow your business." More

Stat Fact
According to the latest Job Demand Survey, the typical salon is a small, full-service business with 5.1 stations and three full-time and two part-time staffers, and it serves an average of 127 customers weekly.

information about Ducoff's Strategies Incubator can be found in Chapter 10, which covers professional development.

A third compensation method, salary plus commission, is now fairly common. This arrangement can help increase business since the hairstylists are guaranteed a salary but earn a premium (commission) for every customer they serve. That can be a great motivator, as is the team bonus, which is paid to everyone on the team if they hit a certain goal every month.

As mentioned previously, you can find a crop of qualified prospects at any barber or beauty school. Check your local Yellow Pages for the cosmetology schools in your area. When hiring a stylist, look for someone who's friendly and has a good gift of gab. He or she also should be patient, flexible, and diplomatic, especially at those times when clients arrive with a photo of a look he or she wants that may not be flattering or even possible given the client's hair type. Since the stylist's appearance is a reflection of the capability of your staff, his or her own hairstyle should be up-to-date and attractive, and his or her appearance neat and professional (although trendy is OK if that's the image you want to project).

Shampoo/Salon Assistant

This is the person who shampoos clients' hair while the stylist is finishing up another client. He or she may also fold towels, sweep up hair clippings, and provide other general assistance around the shop. Often these assistants are newly minted cosmetology graduates who are looking for experience in the industry, or licensed assistants who haven't yet completed enough hours to become a fully licensed stylist. Occasionally a person with no salon experience whatsoever who's eager to learn will present him- or herself at your front desk looking for a job. Those who prove to have an aptitude for the business and are willing to go to school as required by your state can be trained as an apprentice hairstylist. Salon assistants earn minimum wage or a little more. The BLS says the median annual income for a shampooer is $17,300.

Receptionist

In addition to greeting customers as they arrive, the receptionist answers the phone, books appointments, gives directions, cashes out customers, and performs various other customer service duties like making coffee or even hanging up coats for clients. You should put this person in charge of the salon sound system, and make sure he or she is extremely knowledgeable about the salon products you sell.

A receptionist is usually paid minimum wage or a little more.

Manicurist

As previously noted, the manicurist may be part of either the hair salon or spa staff. This professional provides services like manicures, pedicures, and acrylic nail application and tipping, and must be a licensed cosmetologist. According to the BLS, a manicurist earns a median salary of $19,670.

Spa Staff

Your spa staff will be, of necessity, more highly trained and more skilled than your stylist staff. In particular, aestheticians usually are licensed cosmetologists (as required by the state) who hold a special license in their area of expertise.

Some of the personnel you'll need to provide body and skin treatments include aestheticians, massage therapists, electrologists, and possibly a few qualified cosmetologists who work as independent contractors.

Aesthetician

This is one of the most skilled people on your spa staff. Aestheticians hold a special license from the state so they can provide services like facials, waxing, massage, and other specialty body-care services like Scotch hose therapy. Often this person also does makeup consultations and application, especially if there's no room in the budget to hire a dedicated makeup artist. The BLS reports that skin-care specialists like aestheticians have median annual earnings of $28,730.

Bright Idea

Medical spas, which offer services such as Botox and collagen injections, microdermabrasion, and other alternative medicine therapies, are popular and trendy. But beware—state laws require that a physician, registered nurse, or other licensed medical professional perform these types of aesthetic treatments. Aestheticians aren't qualified by virtue of their cosmetology training.

Massage Therapist

Although an aesthetician can provide many massage services, a massage therapist has a higher level of training and additional expertise.

Most states require these professionals to hold a massage therapist license. According to the BLS, the average wage for a massage therapist is $34,900.

Electrologist

This person provides hair removal services and needs an electrologist license in many states. The American Electrology Association (AEA) lists those states on its website at electrology.com/licensing.htm. According to the AEA, an electrologist averages between $25,000 and $50,000 per year.

Independent Contractors

There's one more type of employee who can provide either salon or spa services. The independent contractor is a person who's not on your payroll but provides certain services in your salon, including hairstyling and manicuring. This type of business arrangement most commonly occurs when a cosmetologist rents space from you

---

Passing the Buck

If you can't bear the thought of handling payroll, administering benefits, and dealing with complex tax issues, there's a way out of the paperwork and hassle. You could lease your staff from a professional employer organization (PEO) instead.

PEOs assume the responsibility and liability for many workplace functions, including payroll, employment taxes, risk management, human resources, and labor compliance. The PEO becomes the "employer of record" for your staff and charges you a fee (usually a percentage of your revenues) to lease the employees back to you. Often the PEO can offer much better benefits than you as a small-business owner could ever afford, including cafeteria-style medical insurance benefits and 401(k) plans.

Despite the outward appearance, there's no loss of control over your employees. They still work for you. All that's different is that their paychecks come from the PEO instead of your salon. To find out more about PEOs or for a directory of PEOs in your area, go to the National Association of Professional Employer Organizations' website at napeo.org or call (703) 836-0466.

(known as booth rental) but is responsible for everything from buying his or her own tools and supplies to paying taxes on earned income. Many salons shy away from this practice because it can be a minefield of potential problems, particularly when it comes to the IRS. In fact, the IRS has very strict definitions about

what constitutes an employee or an independent contractor relationship. To find out what the IRS says about the relationship between an employer and an independent contractor, visit irs.gov.

If you want to have the right to control the quality of a stylist's work (since you wouldn't want to have someone inept or careless doing hair on your premises), then that person is an employee, and with that employee you have a host of tax withholding and payment requirements, which we'll discuss later in this chapter. If you're seriously interested in using independent contractors, visit the IRS site to download Publication 15-A: *Employers' Supplemental Tax Guide*, or pick up a copy from your nearest IRS field office.

Hiring Your Staff

This can be a particularly daunting task for new salon owners. You may be afraid you'll make a bad decision. You may feel like you're not a very good judge of character, or you won't know what to ask in a job interview that will help you find a qualified candidate. Or you may be concerned that employees will steal from you or damage your reputation.

Stat Fact
The recent Job Demand Survey indicated that 53 percent of salons had job openings, and nearly 180,000 newly trained salon professionals entered the field.

Obviously, you can't do it alone if you want to be successful in this business, nor can you have a full-service salon without experienced help. So take a deep breath, throw back your shoulders, and let the hiring begin.

Attracting Candidates

In addition to trolling the local beauty and barber schools for eager young recruits, you probably will need to advertise for help. Local newspapers are the best place to advertise since most people are tied to a job by geography. Beauty industry publications may also be a good place to advertise, particularly for management-level staff or skilled professionals like aestheticians. But unless you live in a major metropolitan area where such professionals already reside, this may not be your best choice. You'll find a sample classified ad here to give you an idea what to say in your ad.

Of course, this being the Electronic Age, you definitely need to post your help wanted ads on sites like Monster.com, which charges around $400 for a two-week posting. That's actually less expensive than many traditional print sources, plus your ad will have a wide reach. Other job posting sites you can try include SnagAJob.com, and Careerbuilder.com.

Finally, you can ask your friends and family for leads to people they know in the industry. But tread lightly. One pernicious problem in the salon industry is the sometimes cutthroat competition for qualified help, which can lead to a bidding war complete with exorbitant salaries and outrageous promises. As a new owner, you probably won't be able to offer exorbitant salaries anyway, but just the same, you don't want to get a reputation for stealing away other salons' employees. But there's no reason why you can't make some discreet inquiries. You also could ask other salon owners or employees you're friendly with for leads to people on the job market, but don't be surprised if they don't want to share.

A word about hiring friends: It's usually not a good idea to hire people with whom you have personal ties because sometimes employment situations don't work out and you'll have to let your friend go. Then you've lost not only an employee, but possibly a valued personal relationship. Ditto when it comes to hiring family. They're supposed to love you no matter what, but more families have been divided over issues like money and business than there are dollars in a big Powerball jackpot. Your family and friends are precious—don't jeopardize relationships just to fill a few jobs.

Classified Ad

Experienced Stylist Wanted

Are you looking for an exciting hairstyling career in an environment that's professional but fun? Then Chez Cheri, a new hair salon in Scottsdale, needs you! We offer competitive wages, paid vacation, and other great benefits in exchange for one to two years of experience and a cosmetology license from an accredited beauty school.

For an interview, call (555) 987-6543 today.

Conducting Interviews

Before you actually conduct interviews, you'll want to screen applicants so you don't waste your time interviewing people who clearly aren't qualified. Carefully check the responses you receive to your ads, looking for the level of experience and education you need. Then screen the remaining applicants by phone. The most important thing to ask is how much experience they have. If it's clear the person has no experience or very little, simply explain that you're looking for someone with more experience and politely end the call.

The people who make the cut should be asked to come in for a personal interview. Set up a time to meet to meet them, and request that they bring a resume. But try not to schedule too many interviews on one day. You'll never be able to keep the prospects straight in your mind after about the third interview, plus you run the risk of having the job seekers run into each other as they arrive and leave the shop (which can be uncomfortable for everyone concerned).

Before the candidates arrive, come up with a list of questions to ask. Even if you have a great memory, you should write these questions down, since once the interview gets underway it can be easy to forget something important you really wanted to ask. You'll find a list of relevant questions you can ask a hairstylist below. You also should prepare a job description that you can give to the candidate. This should include a

Interview Questions for Hairstylists

1. Where did you attend cosmetology school?
2. When did you graduate?
3. Are you fully licensed?
4. Do you have any other licenses (massage, etc.)?
5. Where did you work previously?
6. Do you have any references? May I call them?
7. Besides technical ability, what do you think is the most important trait a hair stylist should have?
8. Are you good with people? What makes you think so?
9. What do you do when a client isn't satisfied with a service you've provided?
10. Do you plan to further your education?
11. Would you be willing to attend beauty industry classes and training sessions?

description of the work to be performed, the employee's responsibilities, and the support the person is expected to provide to other employees (such as sweeping up or filling in when the receptionist is on break). Also, include a description of the qualifications necessary to fill the position, including education, experience, and skills.

Before you meet with the candidate, have him or her fill out a job application while waiting in your reception area. You can purchase blank application forms at office supply stores (a package of 100 runs about $6). After the application is completed, usher the candidate into your office and close the door so you can give that person your undivided attention.

During the interview, you'll want to listen more than you talk. After outlining the job responsibilities and your expectations, allow the candidate to do most of the talking about why he or she is qualified for the position. As you listen, observe body language. Is the person sitting up straight in his or her chair, making direct eye contact with you and smiling often? These are signs of a confident person. Is he or she articulate and friendly? These are good traits for someone who has constant customer contact.

Incidentally, it's not necessary to discuss pay and benefits at this first interview. The best time to discuss salary is when you're ready to make an offer, either by phone or in person.

Take careful notes during each interview that will help you distinguish one candidate from another in your mind. Also, write down your general impressions of the candidate after he or she has left. This is very helpful because after a while, everyone starts to look and sound alike, and you're not likely to be able to remember everyone (especially those you spoke to when you started interviewing) when the time to make a decision to hire arrives.

Colleen Blevins-Lunsford, the former owner of Wolf Mountain Day Spa in Grass Valley, California, took the interview process one step further. After first interviewing prospects by phone, then conducting traditional sit-down interviews, she selected the most promising candidates for a "practical interview," which consisted of performing certain spa services on her. This allowed her to test candidates' competence and technical skills in the most meaningful way possible.

After you make an employment decision and offer someone a job, you might consider having a 90-day trial period as a condition of employment. Three months is enough time to observe the employee's abilities and personal skills and decide whether what he or she brings to the salon is a good fit with your mode of operation and goals.

Finally, be careful not to overstaff. While you'll certainly want to have enough employees to serve every customer well, it's better for your employees to be slightly overworked at times than it is for them to stand around idle. This will help your bottom line and increase the amount employees will earn, so it's a win-win situation. You'll know when it's time to hire additional staff by the way sales rise, so in the early days of the business, try to keep staffing levels down.

Getting Your Money's Worth

If you plan to send your employees on expensive junkets to out-of-town training sessions and will pay for the cost as a benefit of employment, you should have a written agreement stipulating that these employees must remain on your staff for a specific length of time, like a year or two. You wouldn't want to go to the expense and trouble of training employees, only to have them leave right away and use what they learned at another salon. If employees you sent on a training or continuing education session do leave—and you have a written agreement about the length of time they're required to stay on staff—they should be required to reimburse you for all the expenses you incurred.

Another way to control staffing costs in the beginning is to hire part-time employees, as well as to assign employees to do double duty. For instance, your receptionist can double as the person who also folds towels when business is slow, and your aesthetician can do makeup applications. Just be sure to spell out all these responsibilities in the job description so there are no surprises (or mutinies) later.

Benefit Basics

In addition to paying a fair salary as discussed earlier in this chapter, salons are now expected to offer a benefit package to their full-time workers. If you start out with part-time workers, you can delay the inevitable, but eventually you'll have to consider offering benefits like health insurance and paid vacation time. Benefits are like insurance for your business because they keep employees happy. The entrepreneurs interviewed for this book all offered some type of benefits to their staff as a way to boost morale, improve retention, and earn a reputation that their salon is a good place to work.

The latest survey by the U.S. Department of Labor's Bureau of Labor Statistics indicated that the average cost of benefits per hour is 29.2 percent, although the amount you pay is more likely to range from 15 to 25 percent, depending on the level of benefits you offer. While that may seem high, the payback is that you'll attract good people who want to work for you, which benefits your business in the long run. Benefits typically offered by salons include:

- Group health and life insurance
- Pension plans
- Simplified Employee Pension plans
- Profit-sharing plans
- Vacation and holiday pay
- Sick pay
- Flexible hours
- Day care

Stat Fact
The U.S. spa industry employs approximately 307,800 people at the nation's 18,100 spas, according to the most recent International Spa Association Spa Industry Study.

Back to School

Another benefit you seriously must consider offering your employees is continuing education opportunities. Many salon owners make continuing education a requirement of employment, and for good reason. Employees who are up-to-date on the latest styles, trends, and products will attract more customers and will be happier because they'll make more money, and they'll feel like they can grow in their positions.

You should establish a training policy with specific goals employees must meet. For instance, you could require your stylists to attend one hair show a year. Not only is this good for business, but employees also enjoy going to educational forums where they can meet others in the industry, and learn new techniques and tips. You also can purchase training videos on customer service and retail sales techniques and have an in-salon training session after hours over pizza and popcorn.

Suppliers are also usually happy to put on product seminars right in your salon. Some of them, like Aveda, hold clinics for stylists and aestheticians at their home office. These can be great opportunities to learn valuable new skills and try new products.

Finally, consider paying to send your staff to industry shows to check out the latest and greatest products and services, as well as to attend any seminars that might be offered. It also can be beneficial to pay for them to join key industry organizations. You'll read about those associations in Chapter 10, but for now, you should be aware that there are many membership benefits for employers, too, such as group insurance options and educational opportunities.

Taxing Issues

Along with employees cometh the taxman. As an employer, you'll be required to withhold several different types of taxes from your employees' checks, including income tax, FICA (aka Social Security), and Medicare. After withholding these funds from employees' wages, you must send them to the government on a strict schedule. You also are required to keep detailed records about the amount withheld and when it was sent in to your dear old Uncle Sam. Your accountant can help you set up a system for paying federal, state, and local taxes in a timely fashion and recording these tax payments properly. For more information about withholding and taxes, pick up a copy of the IRS's Employer's Tax Guide, as well as Publication 583, *Starting a Business and Keeping Records*. Both are available online at irs.gov or at your local IRS office.

> ## Smart Tip
>
> You can find links to the state and U.S. posses-sions unemployment insur-ance tax agencies at ows.doleta.gov/unemploy /agencies.asp. Also, the Business Owners' Toolkit web-site (toolkit.com) provides gen-eral unemployment tax information by state. Just search on "state unemploy-ment taxes" to find the click-able U.S. map, then click on your state for a condensed explanation of the law.

As an employer, you'll have a personal tax bite related to every person you employ. First, you'll pay the matching portion of the FICA, or Social Security, tax, which was 6.2 percent in 2009. You also must pay federal and state unemployment taxes (to fund payments to employees who are fired or laid off), an amount that varies by state; a self-employment tax on your earnings (that's the Social Security tax on your personal earnings since you're self-employed); and Federal Unemployment Tax (FUTA), which pays for unemployment insurance programs. That's another 6.2 percent, although if you pay state unemployment insurance taxes (and virtually everyone will), the amount drops to 0.8 percent. Finally, you'll have to pay for workers' compensation insurance, which pays for medical expenses and disability benefits for employees who are injured on the job. The amount varies by state, and you can find out what the bite will be by contacting your state labor department.

There's one last type of wage reporting task you must undertake. Because it's tax-able income, you must report your employees' tips on Form 8027, and, of course, you'll have to withhold federal, state, and (if applicable) local taxes on them. Employees can use IRS Publication 1244, *Employee's Daily Record of Tips and Report to Employer*, to record tip income. The publication can be downloaded from the IRS website at irs.gov.

One thing you need to stress to employees is that reporting tip income is not only mandatory under federal law, but it's also beneficial to them. According to IRS Publication 3148, *Tips on Tips: A Guide to Tip Income Reporting*, there are many bene-fits to reporting all your tip income, including:

- Improved chances of getting a mortgage, car loan, or other consumer loans because of higher stated income

- Increased workers' compensation benefits in case of workplace injury
- Increased unemployment compensation benefits in the event of a layoff
- Higher Social Security and Medicare benefits
- Increased employee pension, annuity, or 401(k) participation, if applicable
- Higher levels of company benefits, such as life insurance, disability, etc.
- Compliance with mandatory tax laws (Uncle Sam's personal favorite)

> **Smart Tip**
> You can pay federal business taxes online or by phone when you enroll in EFTPS-Direct. This electronic payment method debits your bank account on the day you specify and moves the funds to the U.S. Treasury's account. It also updates IRS records. The service is free. To enroll, call (800) 555-8778, or log on to eftps.gov.

The IRS has plenty more to say about tipping on its website that can help you and your employees understand tipping and other compensation issues for the cosmetology industry. Read it and use it, because the penalties for underreporting are stiff, and the experience of dealing with the IRS can be unpleasant since it takes a dim view of anyone who attempts to get a free ride. So be sure to impress on your employees the wisdom and necessity of fully and honestly disclosing all tip income over $20 per month.

By now, it should be pretty obvious that you need an accountant to help you wade through the morass of tax and other issues that plague a new business owner. If you don't have an accountant yet, start interviewing now.

> **Smart Tip**
> Since cosmetologists generate a lot of waste as they work, you should establish safe-handling procedures to avoid risk of contamination. Some guidelines include placing reusable cloth items (smocks, towels, etc.) in a closed container after use until they can be washed, and washing metal or plastic items in hot, soapy water, then sterilizing them with alcohol or disinfectant.

Workplace Safety Issues

In addition to hiring great staff for your salon, it's your responsibility to make sure they're safe while on the job. The Occupational Safety and Health Act (OSHA) of 1970 has specific requirements that employers must meet to ensure the safety of their workers. These standards are precise and deal with things like the number of toilets needed in the building (one toilet if you have fewer than 15 employees all of the same sex; two or more if you have employees of both genders or if customers are allowed to use the restrooms). You also must protect your workers from injury when using hazardous chemicals (such as cleaning fluids and even perm lotion and color). For more information, visit the OSHA website (osha.gov), where at the time of publication there was an article specifically for hair salons concerning potential health hazards from exposure to ammonia and EMF radiation from hair dryers. There's also quite a bit of general information on the site designed to help small-business owners make their workplace safer.

Professional Development Opportunities to Dye For

Since you already know that the business of beauty is a multibillion-dollar industry, it will come as no surprise that there's an enormous, flourishing professional development system in place that can help salon/spa owners and their staffs succeed in this sometimes crazy, always exciting business. This network consists of everything from trade associations, whose purpose is to inform and advocate; to trade shows, online chat rooms, industry publications, and continuing education programs.

Be sure to take some time to explore these resources when you start your business. They can help you grow your salon, do business better with the tools you already have, and expose you to new ideas and methods of which you may never have dreamed.

What follows in this chapter is a look at some of the best-known professional development resources. This is by no means an exhaustive list—there isn't enough room in this book to cover them all. But it's enough to get you started as you embark on your new venture into salon ownership. You'll find contact information for each resource discussed here, as well as many others, in the Appendix.

Industry Associations

Industry associations offer tremendous benefits like health insurance while serving as an education and networking forum for commiserating and brainstorming. Among the best known are:

- *Day Spa Association.* The Union City, New Jersey–based group promotes members' businesses, enriches and supports the spa industry through networking and education, and increases consumer awareness about spa services and products. Membership is $295 per year.

- *International Spa Association.* This organization represents more than 2,000 wellness facilities and providers from 59 countries. It offers membership benefits like Pulse, a bimonthly magazine; marketing and media tools; conferences; and networking opportunities. Membership costs $620 annually for the spa and the first primary member.

- *National Cosmetology Association.* Founded in 1921, NCA's membership numbers 25,000 salon professionals, including owners, hairstylists, aestheticians, nail technicians, educators, and others. Benefits include personal and business insurance; continuing education and seminars; political action and legislative protection; and a subscription to *American Salon* magazine. Dues are $115 annually.

- *The Salon Association.* This well-respected association of beauty industry owners and managers focuses on the business of running salons and spas. Benefits include business and health insurance; job and career resources; a copy of QuickBooks customized for startup salon owners; a basic version of *SalonBiz*, one of the industry's leading salon management software packages; website templates; and more. The annual dues are $89.

- *The Spa Association.* This comprehensive association provides information, resources, and education for day spas, resorts, hotel spas, well centers, and medical spas. There are four levels of membership, which starts at $199, and includes benefits like a member newsletter, a retail help kit, free and discounted publications, and free spa music CDs.

Industry Publications

Another way to stay current on news, information, events, and trends in the beauty industry is by subscribing to publications that serve salon owners, their employees, and their clientele. Here's a brief rundown of some of the best-known publications that can keep you plugged:

- *American Salon.* Published in both print and digital form by Questex Media Group and available at no cost to qualified salon professionals, the magazine covers information on and trends in hair, skin, nails, and makeup as well as business-building ideas and industry news. *American Salon* also publishes *The Green Book*, which it calls "the most complete and accurate picture of the industry ever assembled in magazine form."

- *American Spa.* Another publication of Questex Media Group and also free to qualified spa professionals, *American Spa* provides insider information about the business of wellness.

- *DAYSPA.* With information on products, trends, treatments, money management, and more, this monthly magazine costs $22 for 12 issues. Published by Creative Age.

- *Massage.* For massage practitioners, instructors, students, and consumers. Published monthly by Massage Mag Inc. The subscription price is $19.95.

- *Modern Salon.* Considered the industry's leading publication, *Modern Salon* is published by Vance Publishing Inc., and covers ways to help salons grow, new resources, services, and networking opportunities. A one-year subscription is $28. Also from the same publisher is *Salon Today*, a publication for salon owners that gives information and tips on how to grow their businesses ($45 for 12 monthly issues). Be sure to visit modern salon.com to sign up for a wide range of free e-newsletters, like *Process Color and*

> **Dollar Stretcher**
>
> The cost of professional publications is deductible on your business income taxes. A copy of your cancelled check or an invoice paid in full is sufficient proof of purchase for the IRS.

Texture Update, Modern Salon Style Watch, Salon Today Business Builders, and more.

- *NAILS*. A trade publication that provides education for nail professionals. Published by Bobit Publishing; twelve monthly issues cost $20.

Trade Shows

Although some salon owners we interviewed for this book (like John Palmieri of Shrewsbury, Massachusetts' Scizzors) find trade shows to be of questionable value ("a total waste of time—they're nothing more than big flea markets," he says), they can be helpful and exhilarating for someone just starting out in the business. Some of the larger shows that might be of interest to you include:

- *Midwest Beauty Show*. A three-day show that features the latest beauty industry trends, workshops, seminars, and exhibits. There were 50,000 attendees at the 2009 show, so this one is huge.
- *International Esthetics, Cosmetics & Spa Conferences*. Held annually in New York, Las Vegas, and Florida, this conference features products, services, equipment, and education for industry professionals.
- *International Beauty Show New York*. The world's largest and longest-running beauty trade show, which attracts more than 50,000 licensed beauty professionals, as well as hundreds of manufacturers and distributors of professional salon products.
- *International Hair & Nail Show*. A multicultural educational trade show with an emphasis on salon retailing, manufacturing, and distribution.

Yearning for Learning

No matter what your age or experience, you never stop learning, and the beauty industry strives to accommodate your need to know with

Smart Tip

Tip...

Many of the industry associations provide online magazines and newsletters that contain timely information about salon management, as well as tips for doing business better. It's usually free to subscribe. Check out any of the publications listed in the Appendix.

Bright Idea

Industry conventions are a great place to network and trade tips with others who understand your business and concerns. Be sure to attend the social events as well as the business seminars for a chance to hobnob with other owners.

a wide assortment of educational opportunities. As mentioned previously, many of the trade shows offer educational forums to attendees. But there are other, more formalized places you can go to pick up a tip or skill.

College Courses and Adult Education

No one said you must have a college business degree to be successful as a salon/spa owner, but it certainly doesn't hurt. If you don't have time to pursue a degree program (or even finish up the one you started back in the day), you can still benefit from coursework in business administration at your local university. Courses that might help your business skills include accounting, financial management, and even business law. Most colleges and universities will allow you to audit classes, or take them for no grade, but you may have to take prerequisite courses before you can get into the ones you really want. For information about business courses at the university level, contact the school's admissions office.

Of course, other curricula can be valuable for salon entrepreneurs. Debbie Elliott of Portland, Maine's, Debbie Elliott Salon & Day Spa pursued a Ph.D. in Leadership & Change from Antioch University, partly because education is one of her passions, but also because she believes in taking advantage of every learning experience possible.

> **Fun Fact**
>
> Bob Jones University in Greensville, South Carolina, is probably the only university in the country that combines a cosmetology degree with the Bible. The Christian school's cosmetology major prepares students to become licensed cosmetologists and offers coursework that can lead to an Associate of Applied Science degree. The curriculum also includes courses in Christian doctrine.

Lorinda Warner of Lorinda's Salon Spa Store in Mill Creek, Washington, held a Bachelor of Science degree in finance and accounting when she went into business with her now-retired partner, who is also her mother. She's a great proponent of a business education. "My education has helped us understand and control the performance of our business," Warner says. "It also helped with the skills needed to do basically everything."

If you're on a budget (and who isn't when starting a business?) or you just want to pick up the basics of financial management or accounting, you might try an adult education class. You never know—you may hit the jackpot and find business courses taught by experts in the field. These courses usually meet once or twice a week for a couple of months, so your time and financial commitment are low. Call your local board of education to obtain a class schedule.

Six Degrees of Learning

The following are six colleges and universities that offer degrees in cosmetology management:

1. *Bob Jones University, Greenville, South Carolina.* Associate of Applied Science degree in Cosmetology Management

2. *Delta College, University Center, Michigan.* Associate degree in Cosmetology Management

3. *Golden State University, Carson City, Nevada.* Master of Business Administration, with a specialization in cosmetic and health-care management

4. *Montcalm Community College, Montcalm, Michigan.* Associate of Applied Science degree in cosmetology management

5. *Santa Monica College, Santa Monica, California.* Associate of Arts degree in cosmetology

6. *Skyline College, San Bruno, California.* Associate of Science degree with a major in cosmetology

Contact information for all these colleges and universities is found in the Appendix.

Salon Management Resources

Salon Business Strategies based in Centerbrook, Connecticut, serves the business information and education needs of the professional salon industry. Its founder is Neil Ducoff, an industry insider who's been a stylist, multiple salon owner, distributor, and manufacturer. The company offers an extensive array of educational seminars; podcasts and a blog, free business articles and downloads; phone coaching; and in-salon consulting/seminars. Its premier product, the Strategies Incubator, is a four-day business course for owners, managers, front-desk coordinators, and key staff. It covers financial issues, teamwork concepts, team-based pay compensation, and more. The cost to attend is $1,295, or $1,895 for two people from the same shop, and the sessions are held at the company's training center in Connecticut. Its website at strategiespub.com has many free resources you can access immediately. Many of the salon owners interviewed for this book are graduates of Strategies programs.

Seminars

For a quick look at a specific topic, try a seminar. You can pick up tips, tricks, and tactics in just a few hours, versus weeks in an adult education or college course. Salon product manufacturers sometimes offer instructional seminars to their adoring (i.e., paying) customers that can be informative. Check with your sales rep for a schedule of upcoming seminar topics.

Beauty Institutes

A number of salon product manufacturers are serious about education and offer far more than just a seminar a couple of times a year. For instance, the Aveda Institute (avedainstitutes.com) offer basic instruction in cosmetology, massage, and day spa operation, aesthetics, and nail technology. These courses are held at locations throughout the country, including the Aveda Institute in Minneapolis (its home base), to educate aspiring professionals to become future industry leaders.

This education doesn't come cheap. According to Leslie Rice of Goldwaves Salon & Spa in Fort Worth, Texas, it cost $5,000 a week plus airfare to send her stylists to New York for Bumble and bumble training. "But people in our industry need these kinds of educational opportunities," says Debbie Elliott of Debbie Elliott Salon & Day Spa. "It's not enough to watch—you have to see a demonstration, copy what you've seen, and be critiqued."

Paul Mitchell and many other manufacturers offer similar educational opportunities.

Cosmetology Schools

This one is more for your staff than for you, unless you don't have a cosmetology license and are interested in obtaining one. You already know that beauty schools are a great place to mine for great, new talent. For a searchable database of accredited schools across the country, check out the National Accrediting Commission of Cosmetology Arts & Sciences website at naccas.org. You'll also find a list of beauty schools at beautyschool.com, which lists beauty schools by state and Canadian province, tells you which licenses are available in each state and province, the number of hours required to earn them, and the state's/province's reciprocity policy.

Blow(dry)ing Your Own Horn

Advertising

Humorist Will Rogers said, "Advertising is the art of convincing people to spend money they don't have for something they don't need."

He was kidding, of course. And the fact is, you do, indeed, have something people need (we won't speculate about the cash-flow part). The best way to tell them about it effectively and efficiently is by advertising.

Advertising is crucial to your business success because it makes customers aware of you—and that's the first step in the buying process. By telling them about the services your chic new salon provides, offering incentives like discount coupons for a first visit, and publicizing the fact that you've transformed what was once a popular pizza parlor (or video store or whatever) into a tranquil oasis of pampering, you create a demand for your services and hopefully entice customers to leave their current salon in favor of yours. If nothing else, advertising will eventually stop people from wandering into your reception area and ordering a meat lover's pizza (hold the pepperoni).

It's especially crucial to advertise in the early days of your new business. Otherwise, you'll spend anxious days waiting for the phone to ring, as Debbie Elliott of Debbie Elliott Salon & Day Spa did when she first opened in Portland, Maine. "I didn't get the word out enough in advance," Elliott says. "Then when I did finally run an ad offering free haircuts for a day, not one person came. Of course, now I have the best customers. We're friends, and the worst part is taking their money. But the early days when I wasn't busy were scary."

Other salon owners have found that advertising isn't very effective for them. For instance, Lorinda Warner of Lorinda's Salon Spa Store says, "We aggressively market to our own database because all other forms don't work for us. We send e-mail newsletters and direct mailers as needed."

This chapter discusses the many options available for generating positive buzz about your fledgling business, some of which are available to you at low or no cost.

On Your Mark

The first step in creating brilliant advertising that tempts people to flock to your salon has nothing to do with writing newspaper ads or radio spots. Rather, it involves creating a flexible marketing plan. Its function is to serve as a road map for your advertising and publicity efforts, gather feedback about the success of those efforts, and help you make decisions about future efforts.

Your marketing plan doesn't have to be complicated—remember, Napoleon was a brilliant strategist, but he was still defeated in the Battle of Waterloo. Rather, it should contain enough information to help you identify market trends and react to seasonal changes, both of which can help you determine the types of advertising that will be most effective. It also should be fluid; that is, you should be able to update it periodically as market conditions change so you're always in touch with the needs of your customers.

The major components of a marketing plan are:

- *Executive summary.* Although your plan starts with this document, you should write it last. In this section, you'll summarize the main points of the entire plan, focusing on your bottom line (i.e., projected sales, startup costs, etc.) and timetable for implementation. The summary should be no longer than a page but might be shorter—perhaps a few paragraphs.

- *Objectives.* This section discusses what you plan to accomplish with your marketing efforts. This might include building business after you open your door, stimulating repeat business, positioning your salon to appeal to an upscale clientele, and so on. By putting these objectives in writing, it solidifies their importance in the plan and helps you stay on track during the implementation phase. Here are some sample objectives for a new salon:

1. Attract an upscale clientele.
2. Position XYZ Salon as the best in the area.
3. Beef up our bottom line by 25 percent.

On Target

One of the basic tenets of business communication is that you should always know as much as possible about your target audience before writing your sales pitch. This gives you insight into your audience's needs and wants, which then allows you to figure out the best way to tell them about your services and products. To analyze your audience, consider the following questions:

- Who are my potential customers?
- Where are they located?
- Where do they get their hair styled/colored/permed now?
- Which services do I offer?
- What do I offer them that they don't get elsewhere?
- How do I compare to the competition?
- How can I persuade potential customers to do business with me?
- Which obstacles might keep them from doing business with me?
- Which merchandise can I sell that will appeal to them?
- What kind of image do I want to project?

You should also include the time frame in which you expect to achieve these objectives (as in 12 months, first quarter of next year, etc.).

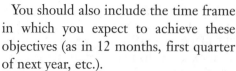

Smart Tip

Your exterior sign is another important gadget in your advertising toolbox. It should be as large as possible given the local zoning ordinances and have unisex graphics (assuming you want people of both sexes to frequent your salon). If possible, erect a ground sign as well as a sign on the building for increased visibility.

- *Market analysis.* Some of the information you compiled in your business plan will come in handy here. By reviewing the demographics of your market area, you can make some assumptions about which types of marketing will work for you. Also, this section should analyze any changes in your market that might influence your business. For example, if a major employer in your city recently laid off a lot of blue-collar workers, your business could suffer if the majority of your customers are middle-class working people. Obviously, these types of situations come and go, which is why you have to revisit your marketing plan periodically and update it to reflect changes.

- *Marketing strategy.* This step is like coming up with a game plan in professional sports. The easiest way to do this is to start with the objectives you've already defined for your salon, and then come up with the actions you must take to accomplish those objectives. To illustrate, here's how you can turn the objectives mentioned above into strategies:

  1. Provide services that pamper and soothe (facials, hydrotherapy) and would appeal to an upscale clientele.
  2. Offer more services and provide the best customer service possible to position XYZ Salon as the best in the area.
  3. Introduce several lines of proven salon and beauty products as a way to beef up our bottom line by 25 percent.

- *Proposed marketing activities.* Here's where you'll outline your proposed marketing efforts. It's like a to-do list and should include exactly what you want to do (grand opening activities, telemarketing to customers about new services, etc.), when you'll do it, and who will do it (your staff, an advertising agency, etc.). It's helpful to put this information into a spreadsheet program like Excel so you can see at a glance what you're planning to do and when the various steps should be implemented.

- *Budget.* Working with your monthly budget figures (which we'll talk about in Get Set on page 138), decide where you'll spend your money.

- *Performance tracking.* You'll want to identify some benchmarks—like the amount of money you hope to make from new retail sales—and then compare your actual figures to the projections. Later, you'll be able to draw some conclusions about the success of your marketing efforts.

You'll find some additional information about writing a marketing plan at the SBA website at sba.gov.

It should be pretty obvious that many of the items you'll put into your marketing plan are similar to what went into your business plan. That might seem redundant, but just remember: Your business plan gives the big picture; the marketing plan is a more focused view. You need both to steer your ship into port successfully. Plus, your marketing plan is just as important as your business plan when it comes to obtaining startup financing for your salon. Lenders will want to know exactly how you're going to market your business since Marketing = Visibility = Success. Coming to the financing table with a sound strategy is another way you can impress lenders with your know-how and can-do entrepreneurial spirit.

Finally, you'll need to include pertinent information from your marketing plan in your business plan. For that matter, you can simply drop your entire marketing plan right into your business plan rather than taking the time to edit it down or condense it.

SWOT Analysis

Before you can determine what type of advertising might work best for your market, you have to understand that market and your place in it. One way to do this is by creating a SWOT analysis, a simple tool taught in business schools for use by everyone from small-business owners to mega corporations. SWOT stands for strengths (characteristics that make you special and set you apart from the competition), weaknesses (things you need to overcome or your competitors could take advantage of), opportunities (anything you can do that might benefit your business either now or in the future), and threats (anything that can harm your business).

Putting these characteristics on paper gives you a clear picture of your salon's prospects and challenges so you can come up with a plan for addressing them.

To see what a SWOT analysis might look like for a new salon in a medium-sized city of about 30,000 people, refer to the sample on page 138. Then try creating your own SWOT analysis by using the blank SWOT form on page 139. You also might consider doing a SWOT analysis for your closest competitors to analyze their strengths and weaknesses and figure out how you measure up against them. Once

▲

you've created your SWOT analysis, use it as a guide for addressing the weaknesses you've identified and refer to it as a benchmark for judging your successes.

Get Set

Now that you have a good idea about the challenges of your particular market, you can develop a promotion strategy to meet them. Again, this plan doesn't have to be complex, but it must be well thought out so your advertising is focused rather than scattershot.

Because advertising can be expensive, you need to set a budget now and stick to it later, no matter what kind of multiple-insertion discounts that newspapers and other media might offer for repeat business. A good rule of thumb is to set your budget as a percentage of projected gross sales. A budget of 2 to 5 percent is a modest, yet reasonable, amount for a startup business.

So let's say you're projecting gross sales of $250,000 in your first year. Using the 2 to 5 percent rule, that works out to an advertising budget of $5,000 to $12,500 a year,

Sample SWOT Analysis Form	
Strengths ○ Five years of experience managing a large salon; eight years' experience as a stylist. ○ Strong business background (two years of community college with a business major) ○ Strong communication and leadership skills	*Weaknesses* ○ No experience managing spa services ○ Minimal computer skills ○ No experience training novice cosmetologists (need to hire only experienced ones at startup)
Opportunities ○ No other salons located within a five-mile radius ○ No spa services other than nails and facials offered in entire market area ○ Explosion in upscale housing in market area; spa services should be in demand, plus can charge more for salon services	*Threats* ○ Further downturn in local economy could result in a decline in demand for personal services ○ Many "kitchen table" salons in the immediate area ○ Last salon owner in town was busted for drug trafficking (gave business a bad reputation)

SWOT Analysis Form	
Strengths	*Weaknesses*
Opportunities	*Threats*

or $417 to $1,041 per month. You'll definitely want to allocate a chunk of this money—say, 20 percent—for your grand opening (perhaps to fund an open house and pay for newspaper advertising). The rest can be used throughout the year on other promotional efforts.

Measuring the effectiveness of your advertising efforts is an important part of your advertising strategy. You should train your reception staff to ask new customers how they heard about you, then log that information either on a simple tally sheet kept by the phone, or on a computer log you can create in Excel. You could also add a column to your sign-in sheet asking customers for that info, but, of course, there's no guarantee they'll actually fill it in.

Spread the News!

According to the salon owners and industry experts we spoke to, the types of advertising that are most effective for salons include word-of-mouth, direct mail, and print advertising. You'll find each of these—as well as a few others to try—discussed below.

Go Tell It on the Mountain

What a surprise—the top form of advertising for salons is also the one that doesn't cost a dime. Word-of-mouth (WOM) advertising is by far the best way to generate positive buzz about the salon. Just think about how often you've been asked by friends, acquaintances, strangers, etc., where you get your hair done (even if you're a guy). It's pretty common for people to seek recommendations when they're looking for personal-care services like those at a salon. So not only can you personally be a walking billboard for your business (without ever donning sandwich boards), but also you can make sure your stylists and aestheticians do great work that gets noticed and results in referrals.

"About 50 percent of our advertising is word-of-mouth," says Daryl Jenkins of HairXtreme in Chester, Virginia. "We do very little advertising otherwise—just some fun stuff like donating $10 to the local high school athletic association every time the football team scores a touchdown. If it's not fun, we don't want to do it."

> **Tip...**
>
> ## Smart Tip
>
> Advertising specialty items imprinted with your salon name and phone number, like pens and refrigerator magnets, are an inexpensive way to advertise. People tend to use these items, and other people notice them. Give them away at your grand opening and throughout the year. The nail files used during a manicure also should be personalized and given to the client when the service is completed.

One way to get good WOM is by influencing what your customers say about you. Some salon owners call their clients shortly after they've had a salon service to get feedback and verify their satisfaction. Don't be surprised if your customers are shocked that you've called—it's very rare for businesspeople in service industries to follow up after the sale. But you'll impress the heck out of them and project a positive image of yourself and your salon. Chances are, they'll remember that friendly call when asked where they got their hair done, and voilà—you've landed another customer.

> **Beware!**
>
> Since word-of-mouth advertising is key to a salon's success, do whatever it takes to make amends the minute you suspect a client isn't happy. Experts say dissatisfied customers often won't say anything to the service provider but will tell six to seven people about their bad experience. You can't afford that kind of negative publicity.

Here's another simple way to pump up your WOM advertising: Offer a referral reward to clients who refer their friends and family. The reward can be modest—say, one free haircut for every 10 referrals, or $1 off a salon service for each referral they make. Of course, this takes some administrative work on the part of your staff to make a referral program work, but the resulting increase in business can be worth it. "Every startup should have a referral program," says Dennis Gullo of Moments Salon and Spa in Mount Laurel, New Jersey. "It's a soft expense that can lead to a lot of new business." John Palmieri of Scizzors in Shrewsbury, Massachusetts, also believes in referral programs. He gives a $10 coupon to every customer who refers a new client.

Bright Idea

As soon as you open your salon, start compiling a master list of customer names and e-mail addresses. That way, you can e-mail marketing pieces right to your customers. But do ask customers for permission to send occasional special offer e-mails. A sign-up form or sheet will do the trick.

A third way to influence WOM is by donating time to do something positive and visible in your community. For example, you could present a complimentary seminar on makeup application for women in a local shelter who are trying to enter the work force, and send a press release to the local media afterward. Any coverage you get is bound to focus not only on your benevolence but also on the services you offer. That can result in significant new business.

It also can result in significant good feelings for everyone involved. For instance, once every three months, the staff of La Jolie Salon in Princeton, New Jersey, cuts and styles the hair of all the clients from one of the local mental health agencies. "No matter how you see the world, a fine haircut and touch of lipstick simply makes it more beautiful," says owner Sasha Rash. "And our staff loves the heartfelt thanks."

House Call

A lot of people groan about the amount of advertising they receive by mail, but the reality is, direct mail is an effective way to reach a large number of people. The trick is to design your offer carefully and use a few tricks to get the recipients to open the envelope or flip the card over to read the offer.

Your direct-mail piece doesn't have to be elaborate; often a simple letter or flier with the appropriate sales copy appealing to customers' desire to look better/hotter/sexier/younger will do. (You'll find a sample flier on page 142). Postcards also can be quite effective. One well-known national department store chain that has in-store beauty salons often sends out postcards announcing perm sales or hair-care product discounts. While there's a cost involved with printing the cards and paying for postage, the labor for addressing them comes cheap—the stylists write them out when their business is slow.

New Image Salon & EuroSpa

Continental image enhancement services for women and men featuring:

◆ *Precision Cuts*   ◆ *Facials and Body Treatment*

◆ *Texturizing*   ◆ *Body Wraps and Massages*

◆ *Creative Color*   ◆ *Hydrotherapy Tub*

◆ *Manicures/Pedicures/Acrylics* ◆ *Hot Rock Therapy*

◆ *Limo Services Avaliable* ◆

87 Kercheval
Grosse Pointe Farms
313.417.9032

newimagesalon.com
info@newimagesalon.com

142

Because they're larger than postcards, fliers, and brochures can be good mediums for waxing poetic and at length about your salon services. Fliers are especially simple to create and are cost-effective—they cost as little as 5 cents each when reproduced by a quick print shop like FedEx Office (fedex.com). They're generally one-sided on 8½x11-inch paper so they can be folded to fit a standard No. 10 envelope.

If you want a more upscale look, go with a brochure. When produced in full color on glossy paper, brochures look (and are) more expensive, which is a fitting representation of the image you wish to project for an upscale or luxury salon and spa. Like fliers, brochures can be designed to fit into a No. 10 envelope (a configuration known as a tri-fold brochure, meaning it has three panels). Common types of salon brochures include "image" brochures, which contain more hype and fluff to appeal to the senses and entice clients to book an appointment; and brochures that list salon services in "menu" format (with or without prices).

You can save money on the design of your direct-mail piece by creating it yourself using a word processing program like Microsoft Word. (Word has numerous flier, postcard, and brochure templates online that make the job easier.) Online printing companies usually also have templates you can customize for your own use. Make the piece as appealing and easy to read as possible by using a lot of white space, call-outs like bullets or lists, and no more than one or two typefaces (any more than that and the text looks messy). Among the things to emphasize in your direct-mail pieces are your (and your staff's) experience and professionalism, level of training/education (training in New York is a big plus), spa equipment, hours (especially if they're extended to accommodate businesspeople), and the beautiful results of your work (i.e., how great/trendy/elegant clients will look). And, by the way, don't feel obligated to give prices in your direct mail. You might want to include prices on a salon menu that's mailed to a prospect list since this allows the piece to do double duty. Generally speaking, however, it's preferable to have clients call or e-mail you to ask about salon services and prices.

No matter which type of direct-mail piece you choose, be sure to include your phone number and your website and/or e-mail address prominently to make it easier for clients to contact you for an appointment or more information. It's also a great idea to enclose a business card with any mailing piece that goes into an envelope since people are more apt to file away a business card for future reference than a piece of paper. Consider putting your salon's hours or driving directions on the back of the card to make it really work for you.

One of the main challenges with direct mail is getting people to open the envelope. Although the use of e-mail has decreased the amount of so-called "junk mail" sent through the post office, most people are still inundated with a lot of direct mail every day. To increase the chances of having your message read, try some of these tricks, which are used by direct-mail pros:

▲

- *Put your flier/letter/brochure in a plain No. 10 envelope that has only a return address (but no company name).* This gives the envelope the appearance of personal correspondence.
- *Affix first-class postage to the envelope.* The bulk postage indicia are a dead giveaway that the envelope contains advertising material.
- *Use a teaser line on the outside to pique the reader's interest.* "Free offer" or "New York runway chic comes to Seattle!" are types of teasers that would work well for a salon. While you can't afford to give a lot away in the startup phase of your salon, don't underestimate the word "free" as a powerful motivator. Offering a deal like one free hair-styling service with the purchase of salon services totaling $75 is a great way to induce more people to call for an appointment.

You'll need to have a good mailing list to get worthy results from your mailings. Refer back to Chapter 3 to learn how to buy a mailing list that can be targeted to your specific market.

One final type of effective direct mail that can build salon business is cooperative mail (also known as marriage mail), which is a package that contains numerous advertising fliers from a variety of advertisers that are sent to every residential and/or business address in a specific area. (Cooperative mail also can take the form of a coupon book.) The fliers usually are sized to fit a No. 10 or a 9½ x 5½-inch envelope and are often printed in full color on glossy paper. The advantage is that marriage mail is usually cost-effective since your insert rides along with fliers from a lot of other paying customers. The disadvantage is that your flier will be "ganged" with fliers from diverse companies like window installers, chiropractors, duct cleaners, and possibly other hair salons. (Or as Judy Rice Mangum of Goldwaves in Fort Worth, Texas, put it, "It's better for oil changes but not our market. We are upper end.") But the low cost may outweigh the disadvantages for you. To find a company that specializes in marriage mail in your target market, check the Yellow Pages under headers like Advertising-Coupons, Advertising-Direct Mail, and Sales Promotion Service.

Black and White and Read All Over

Newspaper advertising is another favorite advertising medium for salon owners. Newspaper ads are effective because of their frequency—your ad can run daily, weekly, or monthly. Ads come in various sizes, like one-eighth or one-quarter page, and newspapers usually offer either run-of-press buys (meaning every paper that's printed will carry your ad), or zoned buys, which means your ad will appear only in the papers that go to the markets you specify (e.g., certain zip codes, cities, or counties, etc.). Ads cost less the more times you run them. The newspaper's rate card can give you information about frequency discounts. Just call the paper's outside sales department, and ask to be connected to the ad rep who handles advertising in your area.

Be sure to select the newspaper carefully. Newspaper advertising is down significantly all around the country, and newspapers are starting to fold as a result. Ask to see the newspaper's circulation statement to get an idea of the paper's readership and reach. You might want to consider advertising in the paper's electronic edition rather than the print one.

Newspapers in larger cities have staff who can write and design your ad for you so you don't have to go to the trouble of finding a copywriter/designer yourself. This service costs more, but it's worth it if you don't care to do the deed yourself. You'll have the final say on appearance and copy and can make changes (within reason) to suit your taste. All it takes is a call to the outside advertising sales department of your newspaper to find out whether this service is available. Alternately, you can use desktop publishing software like Microsoft Publisher to create ads, too, but they require a certain amount of skill to turn out a good ad. If you're game to give it a go yourself, check out the sample ad below for an idea of how to proceed.

> **Tip...**
>
> ### Smart Tip
> Frequency is the key when it comes to advertising success. It's better to run a small ad regularly in one newspaper than to run a big ad just once. The repeated insertions build awareness of your salon, which is the point of advertising in the first place.

Sample Ad

New Image Salon & Eurospa
Full Services for Women and Men

- o Precision Cuts
- o Texturizing
- o Creative Color
- o Manicures/Pedicures/Acrylics
- o Hydrotherapy Tub
- o Hot Rock Therapy
- o Body Wraps and Massages
- o Limo Service Available

87 Kercheval, on the Hill o Grosse Pointe Farms o 313-417-9032
newimagesalon.com

Keys to a Great Ad

Once you've analyzed your audience, you're ready to craft an advertising message that will entice customers to patronize your salon. Here are the steps you can take to write compelling ads, sales letters, brochures, or other advertising materials:

- ○ *Catch their interest with a clever, fun, insightful, or startling headline.* People are bombarded with advertising every day, so unless your ad stands out, it can be overlooked.

- ○ *Stress the benefits of your services and products, and phrase the message in "you-view."* That means to use the pronoun "you" rather than "we" when crafting your message, as in "A day of luxurious pampering awaits you at New Image Salon," rather than "We'll pamper you in our day spa." Then mention the ways your salon and spa can make your customers look great, feel healthy, give them more sex appeal, and so on. You can do this in a few paragraphs or a bulleted list.

- ○ *Create an image of your salon/spa in their minds.* Use the information you gathered from your audience analysis to determine how you want clients to think of you, and then stress that in your ad. For example, do you want them to think you're upscale? Family-oriented? Exclusive?

- ○ *Use a claims/evidence pattern to talk about your services.* For example, if your claim is "You'll feel great after visiting our salon," provide evidence like "Eurospa's hydrotherapy tub will massage away stress and tension and make you feel great."

- ○ *Ask for their business by telling the reader what to do (as in "Phone today for an appointment").* Provide your phone number, website, and e-mail address for easy reference.

- ○ *Use a photo, drawing, or other graphic to add visual interest.* You also may want to have a logo created that you can use in every advertising piece.

While larger newspapers usually offer the most services for their advertisers, don't overlook the small community papers and free weekly shoppers as vehicles for your advertising. People like to patronize the businesses where they live and work, so an ad in even the freebie paper stacked inside the door of the grocery store or library can be effective. Such ads usually cost a lot less than ads in a big-city newspaper.

Advertising space is sold by the column inch, and you can run up quite a bill with repeat insertions, use of color, etc. Your sales rep can go through the rate card with you to outline your options and recommend an advertising buy that fits your budget.

Does your metropolitan community have a city magazine? If so, this can be a great place to advertise your upscale services, as are special-interest publications like bridal magazines or business organization periodicals published in your area. Just keep in mind that the ad rates for these publications tend to be expensive. If you decide to advertise, study each magazine's demographics carefully. If the publication reaches too wide an audience over too large a geographical area, you'll be wasting your ad dollars on coverage that isn't likely to net you any business.

Angela Marke of Andrew Marké Salon in Macomb, Michigan, likes to advertise in high school papers and newsletters, as well as on the backs of the cash register receipts issued by the grocery store that anchors the strip mall she's located in. "The response is awesome," she says.

> **Smart Tip**
>
> *Tip...*
>
> To learn more about the publications in which you want to advertise before you spend your hard-earned cash, request a media kit from the ad representative. Media kits contain information that's helpful when it comes to making a decision about whether to buy, including facts about the publication's editorial content, readership demographics, and ad rates, as well as an audited circulation statement.

On the Air

Salon owners in certain markets may find it's advantageous to advertise on radio, TV, or cable. The trouble is, advertising on these media tends to be costly, and there can be considerable expenses involved in putting the broadcast message together. Still, it may be worth your while to test broadcast advertising to determine its viability, especially since there are radio stations that serve just about any demographic you're interested in reaching.

Debbie Elliott has advertised on network TV and found it to be a useful part of her advertising mix. "We connected with a smart media buyer who has helped make our advertising count," she says. "Our building in Portland is really beautiful—it's a real experience that's different from the other 300 salons around us. It shows well on TV."

> **Bright Idea**
>
> You can stretch your advertising dollars by promoting your salon on the local cable TV system. Since they usually broadcast to a small regional area, placing an ad on the network's local "bulletin board" practically guarantees it will be seen by precisely the people you're trying to reach. Call the cable system's sales department for advertising rates before you pay to produce an ad.

To find out about opportunities in broadcast advertising, call the stations in your market and ask to speak to the outside sales rep. Rates generally are assessed depending on the time of the day you're advertising, the length of the ad, the reach of the station (meaning how many people listen to/watch it), and other factors.

The Big Book

You'll notice we've placed Yellow Pages advertising near the bottom of our list of potential advertising mediums. That's because it's difficult to determine the value of the Yellow Pages for salons. While you'll certainly want to have a basic line ad in the book (that's the kind of ad that comes free with your phone listing and just gives your salon name, address, and phone number), you may find that larger display ads (the ones that are boxed and sometimes have spot color) aren't particularly effective. One could hazard a guess that's because beauty care is so "touchy feely," and a lowly two-dimensional ad (on newsprint paper, no less) can't capture the essence of beauty. On the other hand, it's a maintenance-free advertising vehicle that never closes, gets lost, or breaks down.

One clear advantage of placing a display ad is that your salon is likely to stand out on paper since so few salons opt to advertise this way. Case in point: The latest edition of the Detroit East Area Yellow Pages had seven pages of listings under the Beauty header, which included everything from salons to beauty schools. Only 18 display ads of varying sizes appeared on those seven pages.

But before you reach for the phone to place your ad, consider this: It's believed that Yellow Pages ads are effective because advertisers have a captive audience who have already made a decision to buy, according to Barbara Koch, author of *Profitable Yellow Pages* (FTD Association). "But that's also what makes it unnecessary to buy a display ad in most cases. The real role of your ad is to get the customer to choose you over someone else, and factors like your location may be what actually causes them to call you," Koch says.

A quick check of the phone directory in your market will show what your competition is doing and help you decide whether you should have a display ad, too. If you're still not certain whether you should spend the money on a display ad, consider having one the first year you're in business, then evaluate its effectiveness every year thereafter. If your reception staff is noting how your customers heard about you as described earlier in this chapter, you'll automatically get a pretty good idea of whether your Yellow Pages ad is worth the money.

Smart Tip

Tip...

Always include your web and e-mail addresses in your Yellow Pages ad. There's likely to be an additional charge, but it's worth it since a lot of people like the convenience of checking a website before making an appointment.

Yellow Pages display ads can be very pricey—often hundreds of dollars per month based on a 12-month ironclad contract. You usually have a lot of options when it comes to ad content—logos, photographs, maps, and other artwork are common. The big books also sell full-color ads, but of course your cost increases significantly if you go that route. To place a Yellow Pages ad or for more information, call the publisher of the directory in which you want to advertise.

One final word: Even though we've come down pretty hard on Yellow Pages advertising, don't discount it completely, especially if you don't have a lot of money in your advertising budget. According to a recent Yellow Pages Integrated Media Association usage study, the beauty salon category was the 12th most referenced heading, with nearly 179 million hits. The number-one category (restaurants) was referenced nearly 1.2 billion times, while physicians and surgeons (No. 2) came in at 1.06 billion hits, and pizza (No. 5) logged in with nearly 277 million references. So you can see that people do use their Yellow Pages directory . . . and they're using it to look up hair salon phone numbers. Think about it.

Classic Cards

We already mentioned earlier in this chapter that you should send a business card with every direct-mail piece you send out. But these little rectangles of heavy card stock can also serve as an effective daily advertising vehicle. In addition to keeping a supply in a little holder on your reception desk, you also should distribute your card freely wherever you go, including to people who ask who tinted your hair or gave you such a great cut. Of course you'll also want to carry cards for those times when you're networking at local business functions.

Another way to use your business cards efficiently is to strike an agreement with other businesses that might be able to send business your way. For example, a bridal shop might be willing to distribute your cards to brides (or wedding consultants) who are looking for someone who specializes in wedding hairstyles and makeup. Even a beauty supply store might be willing to keep a supply of your cards on the counter near the cash register. The price for such a service should be low—perhaps a small honorarium or an agreement to send business their way in exchange for the same professional courtesy.

As mentioned in Chapter 7, these little workhorses are really quite inexpensive— only about $25 for 1,000 cards. Always have them printed at an office supply store or by an online printing company for the more professional look.

In addition to giving your salon name and contact information on your card, it's helpful to include descriptive terms like "master stylist" or "certified aesthetician." It also doesn't hurt to mention that you provide complimentary initial consultations on your cards because words like "free" are such powerful motivators.

The Grand Unveiling

Your grand opening deserves special mention here because it's the occasion that will announce your presence in the community and tout your readiness to beautify the world. Hold your grand opening a few weeks after you open to make sure all your equipment, inventory, and staff are in place and working flawlessly before the great debut. To build some buzz, launch a pre-opening promotional campaign that includes ads in the local paper, direct-mail pieces, fliers, and ads on drive-time radio (if the cost fits into your budget). Give the hours of the event, the location of your salon, and details about giveaways or coupons you'll be offering in your advertising to ensure a big turnout. For inspiration, check out the sample grand opening flier on page 151.

On the day of the event, offer mini services such as hand massages or even quickie hair texturing to those who attend. You'll also want to serve refreshments like soft drinks, coffee, and snacks, and pass out promotional items like key chains and nail files. You also might want to pass out professional products like small samples of styling gel or essential oil. (Ask your product distributors if they'll "donate" products for the cause.) Having hourly drawings for door prizes, such as a full-size bottle of shampoo or a complimentary haircut, is another way to entice people to stop by.

> **Tip...**
>
> **Smart Tip**
>
> Place a guest book by the front door on the day of your open house, and station an employee nearby to encourage guests to sign. You can then use those names, addresses, and e-mail addresses to start building your mailing list.

Be sure to have a large quantity of business cards and promotional fliers on hand, and have someone stationed at the door to pass them out to guests as they leave. On the flier, you might even include a percent-off coupon on a first haircut.

New Image Salon & EuroSpa

Grand Opening Celebration

Saturday, September 8, 201x

10 A.M. – 3 P.M.

Join us for:

Precision haircutting demonstrations

Mini spa services

(including hand massage and facial exfoliation)

Refreshments

Prizes

A chance to win a "Day at the Spa" package

87 Kercheval ◆ On the Hill ◆ Grosse Pointe Farms

313-417-9032

newimagesalon.com
info@newimagesalon.com

Surfing for Fun and Profit

No discussion of effective salon sales and marketing strategies would be complete without touching on the power of the internet, that worldwide wonder that has helped entrepreneurs make zillions, allowed shop-a-holics to spend their inheritance money on meteorites in

▲

online auctions, and helped hypochondriacs self-diagnose their illnesses from the comfort of their home hospital bed.

Americans are so accustomed to having instant access to information and services whenever and wherever they need it that you, too, must harness all that cyber power yourself in the early stages of establishing your new salon. But you can do more than just set up a website with your salon hours and services. You can also use the other tools discussed in this chapter to reach out to current and prospective clients to build your business faster.

Fun Fact

The rudimentary information system that grew up to become the internet was first conceived in the 1960s as a way to link the Department of Defense with the military. The "father" of the internet is considered to be the Defense Advanced Research Projects Agency.

Statistics bear out how the internet has given business owners like you the ability to reach an extraordinary number of people. A recent Harris Interactive Poll indicated that 184 million American adults—or four out of five—are online. They surf from home, work, libraries, cyber cafes, and other locations, and many access the web from two or more places. In addition, the same poll showed that at 52 percent, women represent the majority of online users. That's an important statistic. After all, the decision to take the family to a hair salon is often driven by the woman of the house, which means you can't overlook the power of the internet as an electronic pathway to your customers.

In addition, there are many other advantages to having information about your shop online. First, a website gives you more visibility for very little cost. It allows you to post a comprehensive list of your services and prices so your receptionist can spend his or her time on the phone booking appointments rather than just doling out information. It allows potential clients to take a cyber tour of your way-cool salon. It can even schedule appointments (if you have the right software) or automatically send out e-newsletters advertising specials and product sales to your valued customers or prospects.

One of the ways Dennis Gullo of Moments Salon and Spa Hair One in Mount Laurel, New Jersey, has been harnessing the power of the internet as a sales tool is by starting the "Just in Time" e-mail club. On days when business is slow in general or for one employee in particular, he'll pick a service and e-mail his clients to let them know the service is available on that day only at a 20 percent discount. A lot of people who might normally not have tried the service because of the price have taken him up on these "just in time" offers, Gullo says. On some days, he'll book as many as 10 additional appointments in response to the e-mail, which is great, considering that all it took was a few minutes to write the e-mail.

Every salon owner we spoke to for this book has a website for his or her business. (You'll find their website addresses in the Appendix under "Salon/Day Spa Owners.")

Some of the websites are elaborate, with flash introductions and hip music. The overall look of the sites is trendy, chic, and exciting, in keeping with the kind of image salon owners want to project for their businesses.

Apart from the obvious advantages of putting your salon online, there's another good reason to be connected to the web. It's an invaluable business tool for you, too. You can use it to search for information about new salon products, locate educational opportunities, join industry organizations, and so on.

Because so many Americans are online these days, we're assuming that you, too, know how to log on to an ISP, use a search engine, and send and retrieve e-mail. In fact, you may already blog and "tweet." Therefore, this chapter concentrates on the many ways the internet can help you run your salon and capture new business at the same time rather than the basics of internet usage. But if by chance you're an internet neophyte, you must learn to use this valuable resource right away. Virtually every community college and adult education program offers courses that can acquaint you with this amazing resource. There's also a plethora of books and software packages available that can acquaint you with the basics of e-mail, surfing, and even website development.

So ladies and gentlemen, start your search engines . . .

Your Personal Database

One of the challenges you'll have as a new salon owner is keeping abreast of the latest tools, techniques, and equipment in the hair industry. After all, your clients want fresh, fun, and trendy, and if you don't give it to them, they'll go elsewhere. But unless you can figure out the secrets of time travel so you can add a few extra hours to your day, you won't be able to read every industry magazine available or attend every industry show. But you can harness the power of the internet to stay plugged in to changing trends in this very dynamic industry.

And there's plenty of information out there. To illustrate: If you're already connected to the internet, type "beauty" into your browser. A recent Google search turned up more than 571 million sites—up from 20 million when the first edition of this book was published in 2005. "Hair salon association" yielded 763,000 sites, while "hair salon business" yielded 41.2 million, up from 371,000 sites in 2005! Of course, it will take some time to comb through all the sites that pop up to find out which ones suit your needs, but chances are it will be easier and faster to surf for what you need than it would be to work the phones or pore through directories and reference books in a library. Important tip: Limit your search by using more words; fewer sites will pop up. For instance, "beauty salon products" will yield far fewer results (5.8 million at the time this book was revised) than "beauty."

Stat Fact

E-commerce in America brought in $133.6 billion in 2008, according to the U.S. Department of Commerce. And the future looks bright. JupiterResearch, a global provider of information for IT professionals, estimates online retail spending will reach $144 billion in 2010.

One easy way to get information about what's new and exciting in the industry—as well as to commiserate with other salon owners—is by logging into a beauty-industry-related chat room. These chat rooms abound in cyberspace. We've listed a few in the Appendix, but you're sure to find many more when you start surfing. You might try posting messages on industry bulletin boards to find useful information. Salon owners use them all the time for purposes like selling used salon furniture, advertising established salons for sale, or seeking employees with particular skills (such as aestheticians or manicurists). One message board to try is salonchannel.com, which has an online forum board for cosmetologists, aestheticians, massage therapists, and other industry professionals.

Need help with the myriad issues small-business owners face? The internet can assist you with that, too. One place to start is with the SBA's site at sba.gov, where you'll find scads of helpful information like business management tips, financing options, and inspirational success stories. Related to the SBA's site is score.org, a small-business mentoring site that can connect you to a SCORE office in your vicinity. We're also pretty fond of *Entrepreneur* magazine's site at entrepreneur.com, which contains a wealth of information for both the novice and experienced business owner.

What's really wonderful about all these business resources is that many of them, including the U.S. government sites, are available free of charge. But do keep in mind that you must be careful to stick with reputable sources when surfing for information. Just like you can't believe everything you see in print or on the evening news ("Martians overthrow New York Stock Exchange! Details at 11!"), you shouldn't necessarily believe everything you read on the internet. Just about anything can be posted in cyberspace, except maybe websites with content that's seditious or that promotes treachery against the government; web hosts probably would nix those to avoid an official visit from a government watchdog agency. Your best bet is to stick with companies you know whose content you can trust, or whose reputation you can check with the Better Business Bureau, a salon association, or another reputable business organization.

As mentioned previously, the internet is an excellent place to start your search for suppliers you can use to provide the products and services you'll need to run your salon. The really useful sites give details about location and hours, as well as product and services information. This let you make an initial judgment as to whether further information should be requested by e-mail or phone. What you may not find is pricing information. A lot of companies prefer to omit it because they'd rather discuss pricing with a live person who can be persuaded to buy. But you can still accumulate enough useful data by visiting such sites to know whether a lead is worth pursuing.

And, of course, you can't beat the internet for its communication capabilities. From blogs to IMs, texting to Twitter, the internet provides many ways to reach customers, vendors, and other interested parties who might come across your website while surfing. All these communication options are discussed in this chapter.

Working the Web

Just as you'll access other companies' websites for information about their products and services, you'll want both prospective and repeat clients to be able to find you in cyberspace. Your website can be used for everything from posting your hours and driving directions to selling salon services.

"Having your receptionist do the selling on the phone is the old way of doing business," says John Pohlen, owner and CEO of Salon Equipment International, a worldwide distributor of salon and spa equipment. "A website lets customers view your services online and choose what they want the same way they would order off a restaurant menu. It takes the voice out of the sale, which is a good thing because the receptionist has other things to do."

And Pohlen knows what he's talking about. His own extensive website is loaded with equipment pictures and specs and gets hundreds of thousands of hits a day, which means he and his staff can avoid handling a lot of calls that don't result in sales.

Salons often allow visitors to take a cyber tour on their websites. Since the salon business is all about beauty and pampering, it makes sense to give prospects a glimpse of the luxurious (or funky . . . or exclusive) surroundings they'll enjoy with their salon experience.

Spas come off particularly well in a cyber tour. Well-decorated private treatment rooms can communicate a feeling of soothing relaxation even on screen, while suggesting that a resort-style oasis of serene tranquility is no more than a phone call away.

You can make that oasis available with the click of a mouse by using online appointment

Stat Fact
A recent Harris Interactive poll says that of the 184 million American adults now online, 31 percent are college graduates, and 64 percent have household incomes above $50,000. The heaviest users are adults ages 18 to 39, who make up 43 percent of the cyber population. But Americans over the age of 50 aren't far behind at 32 percent.

booking. A number of salon software packages offer this option, which allows customers to select the date, time, and stylist by internet.

"You have to have a website [with online booking]," says Neil Ducoff, founder of Salon Business Strategies in Centerbrook, Connecticut. "It sells for you when you're not there, so when you come in every morning, you find you've made money. It's very cool."

Building Your Site

You'll recall from Chapter 5 that we recommended you consider adding a contract computer consultant to your business management team. A computer consultant who can handle web page development and maintenance will be able to do the programming work necessary to make your site look beautiful (or elegant . . . or funky) and make all the parts work together. Among other things, he or she will design the site's overall look, create the links to lead viewers from one screen to the next, and implement tools like site counters and the online booking option. He or she also can setup the site so you can update it yourself easily. And don't worry—you don't have to be a computer wizard to be able to change salon prices or post newsletters. Your designer can give you step-by-step instructions.

One web designer that's well known in the salon industry is Day Spa Marketing in Fort Collins, Colorado. This spa marketing and promotion company is run by Jim Verrilli, a marketing and brand development expert, who for $2,000 can create a five-page website design package, including a home page and service menu, and product and gift card/basket awareness pages), and spa contact pages. The price also includes strategic page titling, meta tag insertions (to maximize search engine indexing), domain registration, and more. The company offers additional marketing services like service menu packages, direct-mail campaign packages, and newsletter design and layout. You'll find contact information in the Appendix.

Fred Elbel of Elbel Consulting Services LLC in Lakewood, Colorado, who produces websites for companies in many industries, stresses that it's important to get professional help when it comes to website development. "The truth is, most people don't have the technical skills or the time needed to produce a good website," he says. "Your website is an

Dollar Stretcher

If you decide to use a professional web designer to create your website, consider bartering for his or her services to keep the cost down. While it's unlikely you'll be able to barter for the entire cost of a $3,500 website, you could offer to give the designer a certain number of haircuts or spa services plus a cash payment in exchange for his or her work.

extension of your marketing plan and has to be a notch above your competition. Not to mention optimizing a website for success is an art and a science. Most people don't have the skill or time to do all that."

Of course, we do understand that your startup funding might be tight, so if you have an aptitude for computers, and enough time and patience, you could try creating your own web page by using one of the many do-it-yourself web design kits on the market. A web page layout program like Adobe's Dreamweaver CS4 (retails for $399) is a good choice if you know your way around graphics and understand technical jargon.

A web developer will charge anywhere from $1,000 to $3,500 for a fully functional website with links. Part of this cost is based on the number of pages on the site, as well as the amount of artwork or number of photos used, according to Elbel. The more complex the site the more it costs. Future maintenance and/or updates are usually charged on an hourly basis.

Because web designers are often also graphic designers, you can find them in the Yellow Pages, or through your local chamber of commerce or other business organizations. You should expect to work closely with your designer to make decisions about copy placement, colors, typefaces, and so on. Don't just dump the project into the designer's lap. The web page should reflect your style and taste, so you should be intricately involved in all stages of its development. But do rely on the designer's best judgment when it comes to level of interactivity, navigation tools, and artwork.

Content Considerations

Because your website is virtual advertising that's available on demand 24 hours a day, it's important to spend a fair amount of time considering what it should say. The best way to determine content is by thinking like a customer and answering the questions you think a customer would have when searching for a new salon or spa. Here are sample questions a prospective salon/spa customer might have:

Salon

- Do you provide initial consultations? Is there a charge?
- Can you give me the same hairstyle as (name of celebrity)?
- What's the latest look?
- Are your stylists experienced? Where did they study/train?
- What do your services cost?
- Do you sell gift certificates?
- What hair-care product lines do you carry?

- Which credit/debit cards do you accept?
- Where are you located?
- What are your hours?
- How can I reach you?

Spa

- Are your spa employees licensed?
- Are your masseuses male or female?
- Are hyrdo treatments better than massage?
- How and how often do you sanitize your equipment? (important in this age of MRSA and H1N1)
- How long will my treatment take?
- What do you charge?
- May I take a tour of your facility?

Once you've answered these questions (and it helps to write the answers down as they come to you so you can discuss them later with your designer), it's time to consider how you want the site to look. You want it to be user-friendly, yet professional and elegant so it reflects both your taste and the preferences of your customers. For example, are you planning to cater to a younger clientele? Then a funkier and trendier site would be advisable. Targeting the country club set? Then a site with classic elegance is your best bet.

In general, the web page design should be clean and uncluttered, and copy should be brief and to the point. This doesn't mean you can't say what you need to say. But you don't have to tell readers every detail related to your salon business because they're not there to read—they're on your site to see if you can provide the hair or salon services they want. So you just want them to have enough information to make an informed decision about whether your salon/spa will meet their needs (i.e., make them look beautiful, sexy, etc.), and if it will fit into their budget. Save the detailed sales pitch for when they call for an appointment.

Keep the copy fairly brief because many people find it annoying to have to keep scrolling down as they read. In addition, if the text runs onto too many screens, it's harder for the customer to print coupons and other information from your web page—information you hope they'll save as a reminder to call you for an appointment.

Of course, since beauty is a visual art, you'll want to use evocative words when writing your website copy to paint a picture of beauty in people's minds. Here are some adjectives you can use to describe how your salon and/or spa looks, how your spa services will make clients feel, or the overall look customers will get from using your business' services: beautiful, gorgeous, stunning, pretty, elegant, cute, lovely, striking, handsome, in style, en vogue, trendy, fashionable, chic, smart, in, hip, cool, fresh, fly (slang), soothing, calming, restful, refreshing, relaxing, peaceful, serene, tranquil.

Once you have your website copy drafted, you should consider related material that should be added. For instance, you can add links to your online retail store (if you plan to sell items like hair products and makeup), your e-mail inquiry form, and other pertinent information. This is also a good place to discuss the details of the various salon and spa packages you offer so customers have a clear idea of the scope of your services. And don't be shy about publishing your prices—or the entry level price, at least. Clients can call and get the same information, so why not save them the phone call and spare your receptionist the trouble of answering it?

Blogging as a Sales Tool

Websites are great because they provide virtually instant access to information about your salon and spa, including its services, hours, location, and stylist/technician profiles. But there's another proactive way you can stay in touch with customers, spur them to try new services, and just generally keep them informed about what's new and exciting at your salon/spa or in the world of beauty in general: Start a blog.

A blog (short for "weblog") is a short, frequently updated personal online journal. Some people use their blogs to comment on the state of the universe, rhapsodize about their personal triumphs, rail about injustices, and so on. But businesspeople are using blogs to generate excitement about their services and the people who provide them. You can do this as a salon/spa owner, too. For example, let's say you've invited a well-known New York colorist to visit your salon to demonstrate the latest in color techniques. You can blog about how exciting that is, how cool your salon is to be so innovative, how this training will affect future color services, and so on. You can mention public relations coups, great new services, and anything else that might generate new business.

Blog entries should be brief—no more than a few paragraphs at most. The most important thing to remember about a blog, however, is that it must be updated frequently—say, two to three times a week. That's the only way you'll keep it fresh and generate a following that will hang on your every word. If you find it difficult to come up with so much copy that often, consider hiring someone (like a freelance writer) to blog for you. That way, all you have to do is feed her or him some information, then approve the copy when it's ready.

Blogs are either created as part of a website or as a stand-alone entity with its own domain name and address. Your computer consultant can tell you what would work best for you. Although chances are, at this point in your startup, incorporating a blog into your website is probably your best bet.

Social Networking and Other Internet Tools

Although a professionally designed website is your best 24/7 sales assistant, there are a number of other electronic tricks you can try that can put you right in your customer's pockets—quite literally, although in a viral marketing sense. Here's a rundown of today's most popular viral marketing tools (although you can expect the list to change practically moment-by-moment):

- *Facebook (facebook.com)*. You may already have a Facebook profile for connecting with your friends. But it's also a great tool for connecting with customers. What makes Facebook valuable to small-business owners is that the people who visit can post comments, which can be a source of excellent word-of-mouth advertising. In addition, Jason Brown, a Detroit public relations consultant, says that a Facebook profile allows you to get your brand out to a wide audience base in a short time.

    "In terms of size, Facebook is the seventh largest country in the world," Brown says. "That should hit home for any business owner who wants to spread the word about his or her company, its goals, and its objectives really fast."

- *MySpace (myspace.com)*. Another online community where friends connect, MySpace is turning into another business meeting ground. Its features are similar to those of Facebook.

- *Twitter (twitter.com)*. Once you start to accumulate a list of satisfied customers, you can use Twitter to keep them posted on your latest service specials and other beauty information. Twitter is a micro-blogging tool that allows you to send brief (up to 140 characters) messages, or "tweets," via your computer, smartphone, or cell phone to anyone who "follows" you—which in your case, would be any client who agrees to let you tweet him or her. For this reason, you should start compiling a list of Twitter addresses that can be used for marketing. But don't tweet too often, or the messages will lose their punch, kind of like crying "wolf" too often. Instead, if you see something interesting to bring to the attention of your clients ("Did you see Jessica's hair on "Idol" last night? Now rocking Jessica's 'do at Starlight Salon!) or if you want to inform loyal customers about specials or the latest beauty tips, you can send a tweet.

- *LinkedIn (linkedin.com)*. This is a business-oriented social networking website, and as a small-business owner, you need to be here. LinkedIn has 40 million members in 170 industries, most of whom won't be dropping in for a haircut or a massage. However, the site is useful for establishing new contacts, reconnecting with former acquaintances, and even finding new business. In a way, it's like an electronic chamber of commerce, but without the monthly meetings.

At a Glance

Here are some websites you can use to do business better, find useful (free) advice, or just have a laugh:

○ *Amazon (amazon.com)*: Sells books, CDs, videos, and much more

○ *Census Bureau (census.gov)*: The government site for demographic and other population information

○ *eBay (ebay.com)*: An amazing resource for buying or selling just about anything—including used salon equipment

○ *Entrepreneur (entrepreneur.com)*: The premier source for business advice

○ *FedEx Office (fedexoffice.com)*: A leading source for printing and other document services

○ *FindLaw (findlaw.com)*: A legal source with links to information about business and consumer issues

○ *IRS (irs.gov)*: The official source for tax tips, advice, and publications; also helpful: irs.gov/smallbiz, which has a wealth of info for small-business owners

○ *National Association for Professional Employer Organizations (napeo.org)*: The voice of the PEO industry

○ *National Association for the Self-Employed (nase.org)*: Offers advice, group insurance, and more

○ *National Association of Enrolled Agents (naea.org)*: A place to find enrolled agents and learn what they do

○ *National Association of Women Business Owners (nawbo.org)*: An organization that, according to its site, "propels women entrepreneurs into economic, social, and political spheres of power worldwide"

○ *National Small Business Network (businessknowhow.net)*: A useful resource for small-business owners, which includes a blog and offers a free newsletter

○ *SBA (sba.gov)*: An invaluable resource for starting a small business

○ *U.S. Postal Service (usps.com)*: With postage rate calculators, online postage, track and confirm services, and more

○ *ZIP code look-up (usps.gov/ncsc)*: A useful resource for direct-mail efforts

While it's not necessary to sign up with all these services at the same time, they all should be on your radar. "You need to have your name out there on as many service networks as possible," says Brown. "Once you see how they work out, you can pick the two or three that work best for you."

Domain Sweet Domain

Like your company, your website should have a unique name that will be used for your website address. This is called the domain name, or URL. Generally speaking, using your business name as your domain name is your best bet, but keep in mind that domain names must be unique, and someone else might already be using the name you've chosen.

Domain names are registered for a year at a time and are renewed annually. The cost to register a name is as low as $1.99 (GoDaddy.com is one company that offers such low-cost domain names). The leading domain name provider is Domain.com, which provides domains starting at $9.75. Why the difference in price, you ask? It's all in the fine print. Your best bet is to ask your website designer for a recommendation when you're ready to register your domain name.

To start the process of determining whether your domain name is unique and available, just go to one of the providers listed under Webhosting/Domain Names in the Appendix or Google "domain name," then type in the URL you've pre-selected.

Fun Fact

The letters that follow a domain name are known as domain suffixes and indicate the type of audience the website owner wants to reach. The ones you'll encounter most often in the beauty industry are .com, which refers to commercial sites; .net, which is used by networks like ISPs; and .gov, which is for government sites. Other common suffixes include .biz and .us (for various types of businesses), .edu (educational institutions), and .org (nonprofit organizations).

The Host with the Most

You're now just one step away from having a live website. The last step involves selecting the internet host where your site will reside so users can access it 24 hours a day. Examples of well-known internet hosts include EarthLink Web Hosting, NetPass and Yahoo! Web Hosting, but there are many others. Your computer consultant can give you a recommendation to the hosts she or he prefers. (For example, Jim

Verrilli of Day Spa Marketing recommends IPOWERWEB (ipowerweb.com), which offers free domain names.) You can expect to pay as little as $3.95 per month, depending on the host, for unlimited storage space and e-mails. Some hosts will also allow you to register your domain at the same time. You can find a list of the top 10 hosting sites at webhostingchoice.com, as well as the list of domain/web hosts mentioned earlier in the Appendix.

13

Promotion Ploys

Between setting up a website and launching a multipronged paid advertising program, you're well on your way to generating positive press for your new salon. But wait— there's still more you can do. There are a number of promotional and publicity tools you can use to ratchet up your visibility level

e good news is that you can accomplish this at little or no cost,
s a relief if you've already stretched your advertising budget to

s some common publicity tools, including news releases, feature
eauty industry shows, and networking, and discusses how to use
antage.

News Releases

Have you ever wondered how business owners convince newspapers and magazines to write about them? Just lucky, you say? Think again. The fact is, it's not whom you know, but how you let others know what you're up to that gets you into print. And one effective way to tell the world about your accomplishments and capabilities is by sending out news releases.

News releases (also known as press releases) are like little ads for your business. But they're subtler than ads—and possibly more credible to the reader—because when they appear in print they look like news stories rather than ads. To appreciate the difference between the two, think of a 30-second TV commercial promoting a new brand of shampoo said to make hair feel fuller and look sexier, and a longer infomercial (up to 30 minutes) lauding the benefits of and scientific proof about a topical product that can regrow hair in men with male pattern baldness. The infomercial tends to sound more like a news program even though there's a sales pitch at the end. That's the same impact a well-written news release can have.

Newspaper and magazine editors often use news releases as filler material or when they have odd-sized spaces to fill on a page that has editorial content relating to the topic you've written about. They also use them as "idea starters" that can be developed into related or more detailed stories. But be warned—that doesn't necessarily mean the story your release inspires will be about you or your salon—if it gets into print at all. There are no guarantees. Even so, it's a worthwhile use of your time to write and send out news releases, mainly because when they do get into print, they appear at no charge to you. No salon owner can afford to pass up free publicity like that. It also bears mentioning that the more releases you send out, the better your chances are that at least some of them will be printed. In addition, keeping your salon name at the top of editors' minds is a good way to make sure they'll call you if they ever do need to talk to a beauty industry expert for an article.

The outlets that are most likely to use news releases about your salon are newspapers, magazines, and business publications. If you have a local talk radio station or cable TV station, you might want to put them on your news release list, too. Be sure to call the publications and stations to verify their street or e-mail address as well as

Electronic Pathways

While some media outlets—especially those in smaller markets—still prefer to receive or are willing to accept news releases on paper, these days most prefer electronic communication. When you're compiling your list of media contacts, be sure to create a separate list of e-mail addresses. You can easily find e-mail addresses on publications' websites, as well as in media directories like *Mondo Times* (mondotimes.com) or Finder Binder (finderbinder.com), which publishes media directories for some of the largest media markets in the country. Then when you inquire about contact names, be sure to ask what the editors' preferred form of communication is.

to find out the name of the person who's most likely to need the release. Releases addressed to "Editor" or, worse yet, just the name of the publication or station, are more likely to land in the "circular file" than those directed to a real person. Once you've prepared your list of media contacts, create your own mailing list so you have it ready to go when you have something interesting to say.

Getting Ready for Your Closeup

Writing news releases and feature stories and then sending them to the right audience is an important part of the publicity process. But it's even more important to know how you'll respond and what you'll say when you get that coveted call from an editor, writer, or producer.

Susan Harrow, a top media coach and marketing expert, and author of *Sell Yourself without Selling Your Soul* (Harper Collins), recommends preparing a list of six sound bites in support of the main point of your news release or feature article. These sound bites can include anything from additional snippets of information to funny anecdotes. Just be sure to select points that bring the topic to life quickly and in an interesting manner.

Next, practice these key points aloud until you can deliver them easily and without sounding rehearsed. Be sure to time your delivery so you can cover those talking points in 10 to 20 seconds.

Finally, make sure you have high-resolution images of yourself, your salon, and your employees delivering salon services so they can be sent to the media on demand. Then sit back and enjoy your 15 minutes of fame. You've earned it!

The first news release you'll want to write will announce the opening of your salon (see example on page 173). But you can write a news release about nearly anything newsworthy that relates to your business, including:

- New salon or spa services you're offering
- Exciting new product lines
- Special discounts (e.g., discounts available on certain services on traditionally slow days)
- The addition of a staff member trained at a famous New York (Miami, Los Angeles, or Paris) salon
- Special events or seasonal packages (such as a bachelorette party or special "Day at the Spa" gift packages for Valentine's Day)
- Humanitarian work you do in your spare time (like donating time to style hair at a hospital)

> ## Stat Fact
> Ninety percent of news releases never get into print, and not just because the editor doesn't have room to run them. Too often, they're incomplete and full of errors; other times, they simply arrive too late. To increase the chances that your release will run, check it carefully for typos, time it to arrive in plenty of time, and include a photo whenever possible.

For your grand opening release, you should write what's known as a "backgrounder," which is a news release that gives general information about your services, hours of operation, and expertise. In addition to including contact information (phone, website, e-mail address), be sure to include biographical information about yourself (like educational background and pertinent experience) that emphasizes your qualifications. You should also send a 5 x 7-inch photograph of yourself with the release, but please, make sure it's professional quality, not something you took with your digital camera and printed on your inkjet printer or attached to your e-mail.

Your chances of getting a backgrounder release published in a community paper are pretty good since such papers often have a business section that focuses on local companies. But send the release to the bigger players in your market as well since it's possible editors will be piqued by some aspect of the salon and will want to interview you for a feature story.

Writing the Release

OK, so you're a cosmetologist or a business manager because you knew you'd never win a Pulitzer Prize. But that doesn't mean you can't put a simple news release together. To start the process, think about the six questions a journalist asks: who, what, where, when, why, and how. If you jotted down those answers in list form for a release about your grand opening, it might look like this:

- *Who:* New Image Salon and Eurospa
- *What:* Grand opening celebration
- *Where:* 87 Kercheval, Grosse Pointe Farms
- *When:* Saturday, September 8, 9 A.M.–2 P.M.
- *Why:* To introduce the public to new salon and spa services
- *How:* Open house with gifts, refreshments, and complimentary salon services

Now decide what's the most important thing you want the reader to know. That becomes the lead (opening sentences) for the release, and it can be phrased in terms of one of the six questions on your list. For example:

- *Who lead.* New Image Salon and Eurospa will hold a grand opening celebration on Saturday, September 8, to introduce its innovative and exciting new salon and spa services to Grosse Pointe Farms.
- *What lead.* Come to the grand opening of New Image Salon and Eurospa to find out how you can look more beautiful, feel healthier, and look sexier.
- *Where lead.* In a city full of beautiful people, Grosse Pointe Farms has never seen anything like New Image Salon and Eurospa, which will host a grand opening celebration on Saturday, September 8, from 9 A.M. to 2 P.M.
- *When lead.* Mark your calendars for Saturday, September 8, when New Image Salon and Eurospa will host a grand opening celebration for the general public.
- *Why lead.* Herbal wraps. Massages. Facials. You can try them all this Saturday, September 8, during New Image Salon and Eurospa's grand opening celebration from 9 A.M. to 2 P.M.
- *How lead.* Come experience a full range of salon services and enjoy complimentary refreshments during a grand opening celebration at New Image Salon and Eurospa, slated for this Saturday, September 8, from 9 A.M. to 2 P.M.

It's important to put your main point upfront since editors tend to cut copy from the end of a release if it's too long to run in its entirety. Then fill in other details you want the reader to know in the sentences that follow. Just be sure to keep the release short and to the point. The news release should be no longer than two double-spaced pages. If the release flows to a second page, use the word "more" at the bottom of the first page to indicate that it continues onto another page. Use three pound symbols (# # #) to indicate the end of the release.

To alert editors that they're reading a news release, use the standard format shown in the sample release on page 173. Some of the elements this format includes are:

- *Release information.* It will always say "For Immediate Release" at the top unless there's some reason your release shouldn't be published right away (unlikely in the case of a salon); then the header would read: "Embargoed until," followed by the date.

- *Contact name.* Put your name, phone number, and e-mail address here so editors can call you for further information if needed.
- *Headline.* This is the title of your release, which in essence is a brief description of what the release is about. This line should be centered over the text of the release and typed in bold to make the headline stand out. Keep the headline to 10 to 12 words, at the most.
- *Dateline.* This is the city from which the release originates. For example, if your salon is located in Grosse Pointe Farms, the first words before the text of the release begins should be GROSSE POINTE FARMS in uppercase type.
- *Text.* This is the body of the release that gives all the pertinent details you want your reader to know. It starts with your lead sentence and is followed by information you compiled in response to the who, what, where, when, why, and how questions.

It bears repeating that you really don't have to be a journalist to write a release as long as you have good, basic writing skills. But if the notion of writing anything longer than a note to your kids gives you the willies, consider using a freelance public relations writer to produce your releases. His or her rate can vary, but you can expect to pay $25 to $150 for a one-page news release, depending on the experience of the writer. You can find freelance writers through the Yellow Pages, local professional advertising organizations, your chamber of commerce, and university journalism departments. There are also a number of online sites, like JournalismJobs.com, that writers cruise for work, but you will have to pay to post your help wanted ad. One low-cost site you might want to check is Craigslist.org, which charges just $25 to post a help wanted ad for most jobs in the metro market of your choice. Finally, you could use a public relations firm, but as you can imagine, the cost can be pretty high, especially since such firms aren't in the business of writing just the occasional news release for their clients. This being the twenty-first century, you might prefer to try an online professional service provider to get your one-time or occasional writing job done. One to explore is Elance (elance.com), which maintains a list of independent professionals like public relations writers and journalists who can provide writing services on demand. Just search for "writing" or "freelance writer" on the site, and you'll be directed to literally thousands of people who can help. You'll even be able to tell at a glance where the writer is located and what his or her minimum hourly rate is before you make a contact.

Producing the Release

As soon as you're satisfied with the content of the news release and you've proofed it several times, you're ready to send it out to the publishers and broadcasters on your

Sample News Release

NEWS RELEASE

For Immediate Release

Date: August 31, 201x
Media contact: Elle Zebracki
Telephone: (313) 555-0123

*Experience a new world of beauty and relaxation
at Edmund Stanley Salon and Spa*

LINCOLN PARK, MICH.—From cutting-edge hair designs to services that soothe the spirit and relieve stress, the new Edmund Stanley Salon and Spa can help bring out the best in you.

In the tradition of the finest resort spas, Edmund Stanley offers a wide range of innovative aesthetic services—from hair contouring, coloring, and texturing to gemstone facials, spa manicures and pedicures, water massage, aromatherapy, and body wraps. All services are rendered in the tranquil oasis of the Edmund Stanley Salon and Spa, which features a finely appointed salon, a Zen-like grotto with a natural-stone water wall, and luxurious private treatment rooms.

Salon/spa owner Edmund Stanley is a master stylist and color specialist with 12 years of experience who learned his craft in New York City and London. Nor is he a stranger to the aesthetic benefits of resort spas, having spent five years as senior stylist/spa director of the Palm Desert Resort in Rancho Mirage, California.

You're cordially invited to experience the upscale amenities and superior services of the Edmund Stanley Salon and Spa for yourself during a grand opening celebration on Saturday, September 8, from 10 A.M. to 2 P.M. Mini services like hair texturing, massage and facials will be provided, and those in attendance may enter a drawing for a "Nourish and Nurture" day spa package.

Edmund Stanley Salon and Spa is located in the King's Pointe Plaza at 8656 Park Avenue in Lincoln Park. For more information, call (313) 555-0123, visit the website at edmundstanley.com or e-mail info@edmundstanley.com

# # #

mailing list. As mentioned earlier, most editors now prefer to receive news releases via e-mail, but you still need to format it in an acceptable format, which is on what would be a standard-size (8½ x 11-inch) sheet with 1- to 1½-inch margins on all sides. If you plan to mail your releases, white bond paper is preferred, although salons can get away with more creative looks because of the nature of their business. Alternatively, you can photocopy the text onto your stationery as long as your copier makes high-quality copies. If not, you can use a quick print shop like FedEx Office or American Speedy Printing. If the release runs to a second page, staple the pages together. Then mail the finished releases in your company's imprinted No. 10 envelopes for the most professional look.

Promoting Your Cause

As we mentioned, a lot of releases never get published because they're used on an as-needed basis, and the editor may not need your release when it arrives. But sometimes releases simply get lost in the mounds of paperwork on an editor's desk or among the spam in her or his e-mail inbox and aren't discovered until after the news is too old. To increase the chances of getting your release published, call each person to whom you sent the release about a week after it was mailed or e-mailed. Introduce yourself, and then politely inquire if they have any questions about your release that you can answer. If the editor has misplaced the copy, offer to resend, fax, or e-mail another copy. Then be sure to ask if there are specific types of information he or she is more likely to use in the future. Make a note of these preferences so you can refer to them the next time you're drafting a release. Also, ask whether the editor minds an occasional follow-up call from you. Editors at smaller news outlets probably don't mind, but professionals at larger or busier media outlets might find the calls annoying, which won't improve your chances of being published in the future.

Feature Articles

Here's another way to snag some valuable free publicity for your salon: Offer to write a feature article for your local newspaper or other regional publication. The chief value of feature articles is that they can be used to position you as a beauty industry and/or business expert while focusing attention on the salon/spa services you offer.

So be creative. Brainstorm ideas with your staff, your best friend, your spouse, or your significant other, or any other interested party, and come up with a list of ideas that can be developed into stories. The easiest articles to write are informational articles (like the benefits of massage) and how-tos (as in how to prevent your new hair color from fading). The slant you take depends on the type of publication you're planning to send the story to. For instance, a story on "The Top 10 Reasons to Have a Massage" might be perfect for the features section of your daily newspaper. On the other hand, an article about your experiences dealing with the challenges of turning an 1880 Victorian home into a hip haircut haven might be more appropriate for the business section of your paper or a specialty business magazine.

You also should consider sharing your knowledge and insight with readers. The idea is to "wow" them with your creative ideas so they immediately think of you the next time they need a new look or if their own stylist moves to Australia to find himself. So write articles giving tips for working with sculpting wax. Share a story about how a new hair color or style changed a client's life. Or report on great new hairstyles you saw at the hair show you attended in New York. The possibilities are endless.

Before you start writing, take a look at the feature section of the paper or a copy of the magazine you plan to submit to so you can get an idea of how many words to write. Generally, feature articles run anywhere from 800 to 2,500 words, with an average length of about 1,200 to 1,500 words (or 750 to 800 words for a newspaper). As with news releases, you can use a freelance writer to "ghostwrite" or produce the articles under your byline. You can expect to pay a freelance ghostwriter $500 to $1,000 for a 1,200-word article in a mid to large-sized metropolitan market.

> **Smart Tip**
>
> *Tip...*
>
> When writing an article for a publication, always find out the preferred word count, then stick to it. Nothing annoys an editor more than receiving more or less than expected, especially when a publication deadline is looming. Be sure to use Word's word-count feature to make sure you come in close to the required limit.

Submitting Your Manuscript

Depending on the publication, you can submit your article in one of several ways. First, you can create a Word file that can be attached to an e-mail. However, many editors prefer *not* to receive an attachment since there's always the potential for a virus to accompany your inspired prose. So it's possible that you may have to paste the text of the article into the body of the e-mail instead. Other submission methods include burning the article file onto a CD that can be mailed to the editor along with a hard copy of the article, or printing the document on 8½ x 11-inch white bond paper with 1-inch margins on all sides and mailing it. The only way you can find out exactly which form the editor prefers is to e-mail or phone and ask.

No matter which method you use to send the article, you should include a pitch letter that briefly describes what the article is about and why it would appeal to the readers of that particular publication. Be sure to give information about how and where you can be reached as part of your pitch letter.

As a professional courtesy, send the article to one person at a time instead of every editor on your list since they'll be pretty bummed out if they all publish it at the same time. As with news releases, you should place a follow-up phone call as described earlier to increase the chances that the article will be published. If the editor declines to publish the article, send it to the next person on your list.

Newsletters

Newsletters can be powerful public relations tools for salons. They're fairly inexpensive to produce, they don't cost much to mail, they're easy to e-mail (in which case they don't cost a thing), and they can be produced as often or as infrequently as they're needed.

Many salon newsletters are just two pages—usually a single 8½x11-inch sheet printed on the front and back (or designed as a two-page pdf file if they're online newsletters). This size is advantageous because it's cost-effective if you'll be mailing the newsletters, since you can produce it on a photocopier and mail it in a No. 10 business envelope.

In addition to announcing new services, introducing new staff members, and giving the lowdown on the latest hair looks (which, of course, your staff can create), newsletters can be used to inform clients about specials and sales. Obviously, you'll want to tailor the content to reflect your salon specialties since the idea here is to sell your services subtly while providing useful tips and other information. You can do this by adding a tag line to the end of each story that refers to your expertise. For example, at the end of an article about dimensional hair color, you say something like "Michelle & Co. can give you a great new look for prom night or any night. Call us today at (800) 123-4567 for an appointment."

While newsletters often are used to prospect for new business, they also can be sent to your existing client base. This gives you visibility while serving as a reminder to clients who are due for a haircut or other salon service. At the same time, make sure you use your newsletter to upsell or suggest other fee-generating services your clients might be interested in.

Writing and Producing the Newsletter

You can use the same technique for writing your newsletter as you did for writing your news release. Using a concise, journalistic style, answer the who, what, where, when, why, and how questions, and put the most important information first. As before, stating "bottom line" information upfront helps you to hook the readers who really do have an interest in what you have to say.

A word of caution: Don't attempt to write the newsletter yourself if your writing experience is limited to grocery lists or you can't spell and don't know a noun from a pronoun. Nothing will ruin the effect of a newsletter faster and hurt your credibility more than poorly written or misspelled text. Instead, use the services of a freelance writer to compose and proofread your newsletter. You can expect to pay $30 to $50 an hour for a two-page newsletter (or around $150 to $400), depending on the experience of the writer. You also could use a marketing or public relations firm, but be prepared to pay a lot.

Even if you're reluctant to attempt to write the newsletter, you might want to handle the design yourself—with the assistance of a newsletter template program, of course. If you already have Microsoft Office, the best place to start is with one of the 115 newsletter templates found on the Office website at office.microsoft.com. They're easy to use—you simply type in the copy, and the newsletter is formatted automatically as you go.

If you want your newsletter to look unique and special, consider hiring a graphic designer to create a template for you in a software program that interfaces with Microsoft Office. Then you can reuse that template each time you produce another newsletter. You can expect to pay up to $500 (or $30 to $60 per hour) for a graphic designer's services. Check the Yellow Pages under Graphic Designers, or contact an art school to find a designer.

While it's acceptable to design your newsletter with all words and no artwork, artwork generates interest. In addition, clip art is inexpensive and so easy to use that it makes sense to buy an all-purpose clip art package that includes health and beauty art. (Don't forget

Smart Tip

Whenever you write a news release or other printed publicity piece, proofread it yourself, run it through your spellchecker, and then have someone else proof it again before you send it out. Because you're the author, it's easy to overlook your own typos and misspellings, so backup proofreading help is essential.

▲

you can use the clip art on other promotional materials you create, too, including fliers.) Try Googling "hair salon clip art" to find clip art sources. Alternatively, you can try Microsoft Office, which has a small selection of basic clip art on its website at office.microsoft.com. Just search on Beauty to see what pops up. And by the way, although photographs can really make a newsletter look great, don't use them if you're planning to photocopy it. The reproduction quality will be terrible, which will diminish its professional appearance. Of course, if you're planning to e-mail the newsletter, there are no reproduction issues so your photos will look great.

Trade Shows

For maximum exposure in the shortest time, there may be no better place to meet your public than at an industry trade show. These events attract hundreds or even thousands of women and men interested in looking their best. However, several of the experienced entrepreneurs we spoke to said they prefer not to troll for business at beauty shows. "They have a flea market feel," says one owner, "although we sometimes feel like we have to go to see what's new."

All Tied Up

Tie-in promotions are a great way to gain new exposure for your business. By casting your lot with another business in your market area, you increase your salon's visibility and extend your promotional power at little or no cost.

To test the waters, start by forging a relationship with a bridal shop or a wedding consultant. You can offer to refer your clients to the shop or consultant in exchange for them sending their brides to you for skin-care services or wedding day styling and makeup. The setup is strictly voluntary, and no money changes hands.

Other tie-ins you could pursue would be with a dermatologist (since he or she doesn't give facials, there's no competition for the practice), a furrier (for your high-end spa services), or even a health club.

Tie-in deals should always be relevant to your salon. Forging a tie-in relationship with the bridal shop is appropriate; making a deal with a monster truck-pull promoter isn't (unless the event organizer plans to bus all the bored wives over to your salon for facials while their husbands are crushing cars).

Even so, you may wish to participate in a show or two as you start up your business. In addition to giving you visibility with the public, industry trade shows give you a chance to meet and network with a lot of vendors all in one place. That can be helpful later when it comes to ordering hair-care and other products for your salon. The shows that are targeted to a professional audience rather than the public also may have educational offerings of value to you or your staff.

Both professional and consumer beauty trade shows are generally held in convention centers in large cities. The cost to exhibit is usually fairly reasonable and includes a booth space with a 10- or 12-foot skirted table and a few chairs. Since you'll be competing with other companies that offer the same kinds of products and services as you do, you'll want to personalize your display area, perhaps by putting up easels with large photographs of your salon or some of the hairstyles your staff has created. You could even do complimentary makeup touch-ups or on-the-spot braiding as a way to get people to stop by.

If you're interested in building a prospect list for your newsletter, hold a drawing for a salon service. Just put a small sign on your table announcing the prize, add a fishbowl, and watch the entries flood in.

Some of the major beauty shows in the United States include the Global Hair and Beauty Expo, International Beauty Show New York, International Salon & Spa Exposition, and Midwest Beauty Show. You'll find contact information for all of these in the Appendix.

Smart Tip

Tip...

Professional business organizations often publish a directory that lists the names and addresses of every member. Since it's safe to assume that everyone you meet is a potential hair- or skin-care customer, you should add those names to your promotional mailing list for future communications. Just be sure the organization doesn't have a ban on using its list that way.

Networking

Networking isn't just for corporate professionals who do deals over martinis at the Ritz-Carlton. It's also a good way for you to gain professional credibility and respect in your marketplace, while helping you land new business.

Two groups that offer valuable networking opportunities are your local chamber of commerce and Rotary International. These organizations consist of both small- and large-business owners and encourage their members to exchange ideas, support each other's businesses, and barter services. The cost to join either organization is reasonable, and you can quickly build a reputation as a caring and reputable business owner by becoming involved in the groups' public service activities.

In addition, professional business organizations like women business owners' groups, as well as professional beauty industry organizations, can be great places to network.

Open Houses

Your grand opening isn't the only time you should throw your doors open and welcome the world. It's a good idea to hold an open house occasionally to introduce both current and prospective clients to the many services you offer. Set the event for after salon hours or on an evening you're not usually open—say, a Sunday night. Then have your staff demonstrate styling techniques, skin-care regimes, and other salon and spa services, particularly those who could use a boost in revenue. Serve light refreshments like cookies and nonalcoholic punch, have a drawing for door prizes, and hand out advertising specialty items like imprinted pens so everyone goes home with a token gift. And keep your appointment book open. You're bound to book a few appointments right on the spot.

Although you can advertise your open house by sending out a news release or taking out a small ad in your community newspaper, you might want to make the event invitation-only. That increases the likelihood that you'll get more prospective buyers than window shoppers. Your guest list should definitely include your current customers and the guest of their choice. Just be sure you don't invite more people than you can comfortably accommodate in your salon in case everyone shows up at the same time.

Special Events

Hosting other special events is still another way to get great publicity. A few suggestions include hosting bachelor or bachelorette parties and staging fashion shows featuring designs from local retailers and makeup by your salon aesthetician. Naturally, you'll want to send out a news release to the local media giving them the date, time, and details in case they'd like to stop by to have some refreshments and snap some pictures.

Bright Idea

Time your backgrounder news release to go out just before your grand opening. If you're running an ad for the grand opening, give the release to your ad sales rep, and he or she may be able to get the news release into the paper around the same time as your event.

Stylin' by the Numbers

Financial Management

Now that you have many of the business aspects of setting up your new salon under control or at least under construction, it's time to delve into the part of running a business that can make strong men faint and determined women hesitate. That, of course, is the ongoing financial management of your business.

Simply put, you'll need strong financial backing and a willingness to stay informed about the state of your finances to make your salon successful. Although we'll talk about common failure factors in the next chapter, it bears mentioning right now that a lack of financial acumen is a common reason that new businesses fail. Too many entrepreneurs come to the business table with little more on their minds than the banquet of riches they will feast on once their venture is up and running. But they soon find out that the startup period of any business is labor-intensive and difficult, and the early years can be lean. Many aren't willing to work hard and bide their time while their business grows, so they file for bankruptcy and walk away from all the problems—and their dreams.

> ## Smart Tip
> **Tip...**
>
> There are three measures bankers will look at to determine your business's ability to make a profit: the gross profit margin, operating profit margin, and net profit margin. These figures are a good indication of whether you're a safe financing risk, which is why the decision to lend is based heavily on this information.

You definitely don't have to be one of them. If you're made of sterner stuff—and we assume you are if you've made it this far in this startup guide—you'll be able to weather those times when you're not sure how you're going to make payroll, or how you're going to pay for equipment, or how you're going to stretch yourself any thinner to handle the myriad details that will challenge you on a daily basis. And we can assure you that it's possible to handle the financial details of running a business yourself even if you don't have a business degree or even a particularly strong aptitude for number crunching. Luckily, as you know from previous chapters, there are many tools and resources available to help you through the morass of balance sheets and cash flow statements that you must manage, including people who manage money for a living, effective software programs, and tried-and-true accounting methods. Rely on them to keep your business on track and your finances on target.

So let's take a look at what you need to know to keep those financial figures in the black.

Income and Operating Expenses

You probably remember the list of startup costs in Chapter 7 that may have made your hair curl (no perm solution required). Many of the items on that list were one-time expenditures for major things like equipment and furniture, as well as annual premiums for legal fees, insurance, and so on. Now we're going to create an income and operating expenses (I&E) statement, which, unlike your startup worksheet, is a dynamic rather than a static document that reflects the state of your finances from month to month.

While you can have your accountant create this document for you, you might want to try doing it yourself using the simple income/expenses worksheet on page 199. You'll also find two sample I&E statements on pages 197 and 198 that show two hypothetical salons: Chez Cheri, a small salon with four stations, and Jamie Lynn Hair Designs and Day Spa, a medium-sized salon with ten stations in a major metropolitan area. Typical operating costs for these hypothetical businesses have been inserted into the sample I&Es, and you can use these examples as a starting point for determining the types of operating expenses you might incur on a monthly basis.

What follows is a description of all those expenses and how to estimate your own costs.

Rent

This will be one of your largest monthly expenditures. As with a mortgage or lease, your payments are due monthly and are the same from month to month, so all you have to do is plug in this number on your I&E.

Phone/Utilities

There are about as many rate plans and calling zones these days as there is hairspray in Hollywood, so you'll need to check with your local phone company to determine which number to plug into your I&E. Monthly business phone service usually runs $150 to $400 per line, and includes long-distance minutes, and features like caller ID, call waiting, and call forwarding. You should have at least two dedicated voice lines coming into your shop. You might also need additional lines for your fax machine and internet service.

On the utilities side, salons need special plumbing and electrical wiring to do business, and along with these necessities come higher utility bills. Check with your local city government offices to find out which company provides your utility services, and then call its customer service department and ask the representative to help you estimate your monthly bills. Be sure to mention what kind of work your business does when you call (since you'll need more water than, say, an office supply store), as well as the square footage of your facility, to get the most accurate estimates.

Postage

As mentioned in Chapter 11, you'll want to keep in touch with your current customers and future prospects by mailing newsletters, direct mail, and other advertising pieces to them periodically. Unless you plan to mail more than 500 pieces at a time or have access to a postage meter (not exactly a standard piece of equipment in most salons), you have to pay the full ride (first class) for anything mailed in a No. 10 envelope, which is currently 44 cents for up to 1 ounce, or 28 cents for a standard-size first-class postcard. Also, if you anticipate having monthly shipping charges, include an estimate of those charges, too. Incidentally, the U.S. Postal Service website at usps.com has a wealth of information about mailing strategies that can help you grow your business, as well as handy postage calculators. You also can buy and print postage on the site.

Licenses

There are two types of licenses you're likely to need: a business license, which is available through the licensing department of the city in which you do business, and a cosmetologist's license if you're a practicing cosmetologist (no surprise there). If you're an owner/manager only (and not a cosmetologist), you probably won't need further licensing. But some states require owners to be licensed, so contact your state board of cosmetology to find out about your licensing requirements. (You can find a complete list of the state boards of licensing on the National Accrediting Commission on Cosmetology Arts and Sciences website at naccas.org.) Because the cost of a business license varies by municipality and state, we've plugged in a nice round number—$20—on our sample I&E.

Owner/Manager Salary

Here's where you figure in a salary for yourself so you can afford to eat and pay your mortgage while you launch this exciting new venture. All the salon owners who were willing to divulge their incomes (which we have withheld as a professional courtesy) pay themselves a salary, sometimes with bonuses. Of course, their salaries today are a far cry from the amount they earned when they started their business, and some of the owners recalled living very frugally to give their salons the best chance of success. For instance, Debbie Elliott of Debbie Elliot Salon & Day Spa in Portland, Maine lived for a while in little more than a tiny closet over her salon to make sure she could make ends meet. And meet them, she has—her salon's database now lists 12,000 clients and a healthy bottom line to go with them.

While everyone has living expenses, kids to clothe and feed, and holiday gifts to buy, think carefully before you fill in this number on your I&E. A few sacrifices now could yield big benefits down the road.

Employee Wages

There's no doubt that, no matter the size of your shop, wages will take the biggest bite out of your monthly operating budget. The trend in the beauty industry has been away from commission-based pay to hourly wages, and in fact, most of the salon owners we spoke to prefer to pay their employees an hourly wage (sometimes with productivity bonuses). Obviously, the more experience and responsibility an employee has, the more he or she is paid. Wages are also usually based on the local economy, so you'll have to pay more to keep good employees in Los Angeles than you will in Little Rock. For guidance, refer back to Chapter 9 for typical compensation rates; this should give you an idea how much to budget for. For the sake of our hypothetical I&E calculations, we've used the following wages (most courtesy of the U.S. Bureau of Labor Statistics):

- Owner: $35,000 per year (salaried)
- Manager: $30,000 per year (salaried)
- Massage therapist: $16/hour
- Aesthetician: $12/hour
- Hairstylist/cosmetologist: $11/hour
- Manicurist: $9.50/hour
- Receptionist: $9/hour
- Shampooer: $8/hour
- Maintenance: $13/hour

Benefits/Taxes

Benefits are another expense that will eat up a lot of your monthly income, but as you know, happy employees are productive employees, so benefits are a necessity. So are taxes, since a happy government is one that won't garnish your wages or take your house and car to pay for back taxes.

ABLS study showed that in 2009, benefits constituted 29.2 percent of total employee compensation. However, using that number would put you in a league with the giants of industry. You're more likely to pay 15 to 25 percent, but you can allot even less if that's all you can afford. For the sake of having a number to work with, multiply the figure you used on the employee wages line of your I&E by 0.15.

Figuring out the tax portion of the amount on the benefits/tax line is a little trickier. As you know from Chapter 9, there's a whole laundry list of taxes Uncle Sam expects you to collect from your employees, including income tax on wages and tips, FICA, and Medicare. But the only part you need to be concerned with for your I&E is the slew of employer taxes you're responsible for, including the matching portion of the FICA, federal, and state unemployment insurance (UI) taxes, Federal Unemployment Tax (FUTA), and workers' compensation insurance. Unfortunately, there's not a simple formula for estimating state UI or workers' comp insurance

Beware!
Employee theft is a reality. Signs of theft can include coins placed in the wrong cash register slots, paper clips in coin slots, and bills turned upside down, or with the presidents' heads pointing the opposite way from the other bills. These "markers" help dishonest employees track how much they've shorted the register so the amount can be stolen later.

because they vary by state, plus in the case of state UI, the rates themselves vary depending on your payroll amount and other incomprehensible factors. Since you don't have previous records to compare to, you should estimate high so you're not caught short. It will be easier to make a good estimate next year once you have a year's worth of records to support it. Better still, find an experienced accountant fast to advise you properly.

For the sake of this exercise, we've used a tax rate of 12 percent which includes FICA at 6.2 percent, FUTA at 0.8 percent, and 5 percent (estimated) for UI and workers' comp. You may recall from an earlier discussion that business owners aren't covered by workers' comp, but we're including the owners' salaries in the I&E calculations anyway as a way to estimate the overall taxes on the high side.

Once you've calculated both the benefits and the tax figures, add them together, divide by 12, and enter that figure in the benefits/tax category.

Advertising/Promotion

Here's where you'll estimate the cost of producing and printing brochures, newsletters, and other advertising or promotion pieces you may decide to send out. Yellow Pages advertising and the costs incurred for special events, like open houses, also go here.

Legal Services

This is one of those categories where you may or may not have monthly expenses. As mentioned in Chapter 5, some attorneys work on retainers, in which case you would include one-twelfth of that figure each month on your I&E. If your attorney works on a project basis, you might want to guesstimate the number of hours you'll need his or her services, multiply that by the attorney's hourly rate, and include one-twelfth of that amount on your I&E. If you're going with a package of basic startup services and don't anticipate using the attorney much after that, include the entire amount on your startup worksheet and not on your I&E. You can always add a dollar figure into the "Miscellaneous" category later if an unexpected legal fee pops up.

Accounting Services

It was also mentioned in Chapter 5 that it's wise to secure the services of an accountant for your salon. You can certainly do the basic bookkeeping yourself using QuickBooks or Peachtree, but for the more complex accounting chores (including business taxes), it's best to rely on an accountant since he or she knows the ins and outs of debits and credits, and all those other mysterious numbers that show up on ledgers. Accountants usually work on an hourly basis, so find out his or her rate, multiply that by a reasonable number of hours, and use that figure on your I&E.

Office and Salon Supplies

This is a big category—so big, in fact, that you might want to divide it into two parts. Your hair-care and beauty supplies, including shampoo, mousse, cotton coils, perms, and everything else listed in Chapter 7, make up one part; paper clips, stationery, business cards, and all the other office supplies you need to do business every day constitute the second part. Obviously, some of these supplies, like business printing, won't be incurred every month, but you still want them to appear on your I&E. So use the figures you got when you priced out supplies like stationery or business cards and divide them by 12. Add these numbers to the other fixed costs you've estimated for the month to arrive at a bottom-line figure.

Beware!

If you use your personal vehicle for salon business, you might be able to deduct a percentage of the vehicle payment, as well as gasoline and insurance costs on your income taxes. However, the IRS requires a written record of the miles driven that's broken down into business, personal and volunteer mileage. Office supply stores sell mileage log books that can be used to satisfy the government's need to know.

Maintenance

If you're leasing your building or other retail space, chances are exterior work like snow removal or grass cutting will be included as part of your monthly lease. But if you're buying a building, make sure you include these costs on your I&E. If you're paying only for snow removal for, say, five months of the year, add up the cost for those five months, divide it by 12, and plug that figure into your spreadsheet.

The other maintenance cost that's commonly incurred by salon owners is for interior maintenance. This may include, but is not limited to: emptying trash, sweeping and washing floors, dusting, and possibly washing and folding towels, capes, and other items. Some owners make this the responsibility of their employees, but it may also be a good idea to hire a professional cleaning company that specializes in commercial facilities to make sure the salon is really clean. These companies charge by the hour or by the square foot, and you usually can have them come in as often as you like, from daily to weekly or even biweekly.

Cleanliness pays, according to Daryl Jenkins of HairXtreme in Chester, Virginia. "Clients notice how clean our salon is," he says, "and that gives the staff pride in their workplace."

Insurance

Using the worksheet on page 199, tally up the dollar amount needed to buy enough insurance to give you peace of mind in the face of most risk management situations, and then divide that figure by 12. Since it's unlikely that you'll use your vehicle for salon business, we haven't included auto insurance on our sample I&Es.

Magazine Subscriptions

You're bound to want to subscribe to a number of publications, from consumer magazines that show trendy hairstyles to periodicals and newsletters that can help you run your business better. All these publications (you'll find descriptions of some of them in Chapter 10), as well as the hairstyle books you'll want to leave in your waiting area for customers who want a new look, are legitimate business expenses and should be included on your I&E.

Membership Dues

Among the types of membership dues you'll want to include here are the costs to join beauty industry organizations, hair industry associations, and local business organizations like the chamber of commerce. Refer back to Chapter 10 for a list of the major salon and spa organizations.

Loan Repayment

This one doesn't need much explanation. If you financed your equipment or made building improvements that aren't included in your monthly mortgage payment, you'll have a figure to include on your I&E—and it's likely to have a place of honor there for a very long time. This category also includes loans you obtain from family, friends, and investors (discussed later in this chapter).

Take the Money (But Don't Run Yet)

An important monthly expense you'll incur will be point-of-sale processing costs for accepting Visa, MasterCard, and other credit cards, as well as debit cards. The rates vary among the many merchant account services, and the list of potential fees is staggering. For example, here's the list of fees Merchant Accounts Express (merchantexpress.com), a provider of internet merchant accounts, says you might encounter:

- ○ ACH fee or daily batch fee
- ○ Address verification service fee
- ○ Annual fee
- ○ Application/setup fee
- ○ Cancellation or termination fee
- ○ Chargeback/retrieval fee
- ○ Discount rate
- ○ Hidden or junk fees
- ○ Internet gateway fee
- ○ Monthly minimum fee
- ○ Monthly statement/support/service fee
- ○ PIN debit transaction fees
- ○ Reprogramming fee
- ○ Surcharge/partially-qualified/nonqualified fees
- ○ Transaction fees
- ○ Voice authorization fee

Fortunately, you're not likely to have to pay every one of these fees—and in fact, you should run away really fast if you're ever presented with a list like this by an eager merchant account provider. Instead, you're more likely to have to pay the types of fees Merchant Express charges, including a monthly statement fee ($10–15); a retail discount rate of 1.69 percent (meaning you pay the merchant account company 1.69 percent of each transaction); and a transaction retail transaction/batch fee of 19 cents per transaction. Be sure to shop around carefully for the best deal—and don't forget to check the bank that provides your business checking account to see if it offers merchant services. It probably does.

Take the Money (But Don't Run Yet), continued

You'll find a list of merchant account providers in the Appendix to check out.

If you're planning to accept personal checks (which is now considered a non-traditional form of payment), a check verification service is also a good idea because it can reduce your risk of accepting a bad check. The cost is similar to that of a merchant account and usually includes a discount fee on all checks you accept (usually around 1.5 percent, according to MerchantSeek.com), a per-transaction fee of 10 to 35 cents, and possibly a monthly minimum fee, a statement fee, and an application fee. But what you get is the best possible verification that every check you accept is good. Again, it pays to shop around for the best rates.

Online Service Fees

This one is easy to predict since you'll sign up for internet service at a set price. High-speed cable service (aka broadband) is the most expensive at about $40–50 a month, but the blazing speed makes the cost worth it. A DSL line will cost $30–40 for basic service, while a standard (read: slow) dial-up line is $20–25 per month. Web hosting charges can be as low as $4.99 per month (GoDaddy.com offers service at this price), but $8.95 a month is average. That cost also goes on your I&E.

Miscellaneous Expenses

Finally, other incidentals like flowers for the reception desk or light refreshments for the monthly staff meeting can go in this category. Using a figure that's 10 percent of your total expenses is usually sufficient.

Forecasting Receivables

Now that you've gone through the somewhat depressing exercise of calculating how much of the money that comes in each month will flutter off to your creditors, you can estimate how much money you'll need to earn to stay solvent and—yeah!—make a profit.

Let's use Chez Cheri as an example of how to do a rudimentary estimate. If the four-station salon's total expenses for the month are approximately $9,000, and Cheri charges $30 for a haircut, she and/or her staff has to shear 300 heads just to break even. Of course, because she's a color expert and she charges more for color than she does for haircuts, Cheri will make a profit if she does color services for, say, a third of those customers rather than just cutting their hair. So, of course, Cheri will probably want to use her advertising dollars to promote her color services, as well as any other services that bring in extra dough.

Now it's your turn. Figure out the dollar amount of services (based on factors like the number of haircuts or perms you'll have to do) to get a round number. Then, armed with this information, you can go on to the next step, which is tracking your receivables and sending them into battle against your expenses.

Smart Tip

Tip...

It's important to reconcile your accounts at the end of each business day. The total of the cash in the till, credit card slips, debit transactions, and checks should equal the amount of money you started with at the beginning of the day plus all the sales recorded on the till. A salon software program like Unique Salon Software (from $395) will easily calculate these totals for you and help you find shortages.

Bookkeeping Solutions

Although your accountant is likely to become one of your closest friends while you're in business, there's no reason you can't do some of the basic accounting yourself using one of the accounting software packages on the market. These packages are both affordable and user-friendly, so even people who are financially challenged can use them. Another good reason to handle some of the basic accounting tasks is so you always have a good idea of how the business is doing so you can make adjustments along the way.

Beware!

If you can't reconcile your books at the end of the day, you've probably made an arithmetic error or input something incorrectly in your accounting software. However, if you consistently have shortages in the register that you can't find, you could have a problem with employee theft. Check and recheck the calculations before you accuse anyone.

Without exception, the salon pros we interviewed used QuickBooks Pro by Intuit. It retails for $199.95 (although you can find it discounted at places like Amazon.com) and allows you to create invoices, track receivables, write checks, and pay bills. It also interfaces with Microsoft Excel, Quicken, and Microsoft Accounting, and offers add-on merchant account and payroll services and more. You can find QuickBooks at office supply and computer stores.

Another popular accounting package you might like to try is Peachtree by Sage Pro Accounting. It retails for $199.95 and is available online, from computer stores, and directly from Peachtree (peachtree.com).

Tip...

Smart Tip

One of the best reasons to use accounting software is because it prevents inadvertent math errors. All you have to do is plug in the right numbers, and they'll tally up correctly. If you've ever footed the same column of numbers three times and arrived at three different totals, you understand the value of such accuracy.

The salon software packages usually include their own accounting programs and may be fine for following your finances. But since your accountant isn't likely to be able to access your data without having the same software, you might want to stick with one of the more common accounting packages.

Financing 101

The moment of truth has arrived: You're ready to put together the financing you need to launch this grand enterprise. While operating capital can come from a number of sources, the most common ones for salon owners are conventional lenders; friends and family; personal savings; and government agencies.

Banks

This is where most new business owners go to raise capital. Considering that your business plan has been whipped into shape, your marketing plan sings, and your startup costs look both reasonable and feasible, it should be a snap to convince a banker that you're a good risk, right?

Wrong.

"Banks don't like the salon industry," says Dennis Gullo of Moments Salon and Spa Hair One in Mount Laurel, New Jersey. "There's an overall negative perception that salons aren't serious businesses, which is ridiculous since many salons are very sophisticated with sophisticated business systems."

In addition, bankers are often reluctant to take a chance on small-business startups like salons because they don't have a track record of success. Worse yet, large banks are often more interested in funding big companies because they usually require bigger loans and use more fee-generating services than a small business does.

Tip...

Smart Tip

Since your personal credit will determine your creditworthiness, you should request a copy of your credit report from any of the three major credit bureaus in the United States before applying for financing. Then check to verify that your credit report is correct since experts say that up to 25 percent of Americans find errors in their files.

Credit Where Credit Is Due

Using your personal credit cards to charge some of your startup costs can save you both the hassle of applying for a bank loan and the hefty costs that can be associated with it. Of course, the downside is that you'll probably pay interest rates of as much as 24.9 percent. So if you decide to use plastic, use a card with the lowest interest rate. Watch your mailbox for offers from lenders with variable rates as low as 3.9 percent.

Alternatively, you may be able to obtain a separate business line of credit through your credit card company. This allows you to borrow as much as $100,000 at a rate that's probably a lot less than what your bank would charge for a similar line of credit. American Express is one company that offers this type of line of credit, with small-business limits of $50,000. Its Business Line of Credit doesn't require collateral, and the adjustable rate at publication time was prime plus 1.99 percent for both cash and purchases, although it can sneak up to as much as prime plus 6.99 percent when you're not looking.

But all is not lost. You just need to shop around to find the bank that will welcome the opportunity to work with you. Chances are, it will be a small community bank.

"Small-business owners usually do better by selecting a bank with a community banking philosophy," says Robert Sisson, author of *Show Me the Money*. "These are the banks that support their communities and function almost as much as a consultant as a bank."

Since banks are highly competitive, even in a depressed economy, and often advertise for new business, you probably already know which banks in your community have a community-based philosophy. To find out whether the bank you're interested in is entrepreneur-friendly, check out its annual report, which is usually readily available at branch offices. Look for clues about its financial focus and business outlook. Generally speaking, an institution that supports minority- and women-owned businesses is

Fun Fact

All banks use certain factors to determine a business's creditworthiness, known in banking circles as the "four Cs." These criteria include:

1. Condition (profitability of the industry in general and your company in particular)
2. Collateral (sufficient personal property that's pledged to secure the loan)
3. Character (the owner's personal credit history)
4. Capacity (ability to repay the debt)

likely to be willing to work with a small-business owner even if you personally are not a minority or a woman. Other information you'll want to check is the number of loans the bank makes to small companies, since this is a pretty good indicator of its commitment to the community, as well as its overall business mix and the industries it serves.

All banks, no matter how large, require collateral to secure loans. Acceptable forms of collateral may include your savings account, life insurance policy (if it has cash value), or hard assets (including your equipment, inventory, vehicles, and real estate). Bankers are skilled at estimating the value of hard assets and can tell you whether the collateral you offer will hold its value during the life of the loan and thus is sufficient to secure it.

Incidentally, it bears repeating that it can be difficult to obtain operating capital if you don't have a track record of success. This is particularly true when it comes to service businesses like a salon, where the greatest equity tends to be in talent and hard work. Therefore, seek financing for tangibles like real estate or equipment, and if possible rely on the other sources that follow to cover operating expenses.

And by the way, while you're at the bank, open a business checking account. It's necessary to keep your personal and business finances separate.

Life Savings

For many entrepreneurs, using personal savings is the fastest and best way to get a business up and running—assuming, of course, that your life savings amount to more than just a modest nest egg. If you decide to go this route, consider every source of personal capital you may have, including savings accounts and certificates of deposit; income tax refunds; stocks and bonds; savings bonds; real estate, vehicles, and personal assets like jewelry (all of which can be sold to raise cash); and retirement funds like pension plans, IRAs, 401(k) plans, SEPs, and Keoghs. A lot of people prefer not to touch retirement plan funds because there's a penalty for cashing out before age 59½. But if your salon is successful, you can easily recoup those penalties, so raiding the pension funds may be a wise choice.

Angela Marke and her partner, Andrew Bernard, came up with $100,000 each and funded their Macomb, Michigan salon, Andrew Marké Salon, totally out of personal savings (mostly stocks and mutual funds) because they didn't want to owe any money. On the other hand, HairXtreme was founded on far less—about $33,000, according to Daryl Jenkins, whose wife, Shannon, started the salon in 1998.

"Shannon started small, with four stations, a reception desk, a cash register, retail products, professional-use supplies, and shampoo bowls," Jenkins says. "She used $35 bookcases to display retail products and as back bars."

All in the Family

Another viable source of capital is family and friends who are supportive of your venture. While it can be difficult and downright humbling to ask loved ones and pals for money, chances are they'll be willing to help and will offer more flexible repayment plans. Just be sure if you tap them for funds that you structure the loan as a legitimate business transaction with interest. No verbal or handshake agreements here. Put everything down on paper, including interest and repayment terms, and then live by the terms of the agreement. This is particularly important when it comes to borrowing from family members since they're often more forgiving because they want you to be successful, but there can be hard feelings that last a lifetime if something goes awry.

Beware!

If you don't have a written loan agreement when you borrow money from friends and family, the IRS is likely to consider those funds to be a gift rather than a loan. As a result, your benefactors could be socked with a huge tax bill in exchange for their benevolence.

Also, don't pledge to repay out of profits only. Include your loan repayment on your monthly I&E as discussed earlier so your creditors always get paid first. Otherwise, you run the risk of destroying relationships—something you absolutely can't afford to do at a time when you need moral support the most. Besides, your new business is important, but your family and friends are priceless. Protect them just like you would your business assets.

Pat Millar wisely did just that when she borrowed $15,000 from her father to launch her Clinton, New Jersey salon. It was enough cash to lease her first location, and buy salon chairs, equipment, and supplies. She paid him back with interest, just like it was a bank loan.

Your Tax Dollars at Work

Your friendly U.S. government is yet another source of fiscal support. Uncle Sam has numerous agencies that offer assistance in the form of direct loans, guaranteed loans, and grants to small-business owners who otherwise might not have a chance to spread their entrepreneurial wings.

Chief among those federal agencies is the SBA, which is considered the last resort for business owners who can't qualify for conventional bank loans. Although the SBA doesn't offer direct loans, it does offer a small-business guaranteed loan program, in which a bank or other lending institution provides the cash, and the loan is guaranteed partially by the SBA and partially by the lender.

In addition to filling out a lengthy application package (a mere application isn't enough), you must also meet the SBA's definition of a small business, which includes private ownership and operation of the business, lack of financial resources to self-fund the business, and other eligibility criteria. The loan carries a guarantee fee starting at 2 percent and other fees.

The SBA also offers financial advice, counseling, and training. For more information, check the SBA's website at sba.gov, e-mail answerdesk@sba.gov, or call the answer desk at (800) 8-ASK-SBA.

Other federal agencies that may be able to help you finance your startup salon include the Minority Business Development Agency (mbda.gov), which assists minority business owners and offers federal grants and loans; and the Small Business Investment Company program (nasbic.org), which consists of privately organized and managed venture capital firms that are licensed by the SBA to make equity capital or long-term loans.

All the financing methods discussed in this chapter are fairly traditional, but the entrepreneurs interviewed for this book came up with other creative ways to get into business. For instance, Lorinda Warner in Mill Creek, Washington, financed her startup in 1984 using funds generated when her parents took out a second mortgage on their home. To launch his salon, Scizzors, John Palmieri in Shrewsbury, Massachusetts, sold his car and used $10,000 in personal savings. Then he and his partner at the time borrowed $2,500 each from one bank, and later the same day borrowed another $2,500 each from another bank.

Sample Operating Income/Expenses

Here are sample operating income/expense statements for two hypothetical salons that reflect typical operating costs for the industry. Chez Cheri (below) has four chairs, while Jamie Lynn Hair Designs and Day Spa (see page 198) has ten. You can compute your own projected income and expenses using the worksheet provided on page 199.

Chez Cheri

Projected Monthly Income	**$12,000**
Projected Monthly Expenses	
Rent/mortgage	$1,000
Phone	$80
Utilities	$200
Postage	$25
Owner/manager salary	$2,000
Employee wages	$5,000
Benefits/taxes	$600
Advertising/promotion	$200
Legal services	
Licenses	$20
Accounting services	$120
Supplies	$100
Maintenance	$200
Insurance	$100
Magazine subscriptions	$5
Membership dues	$10
Loan repayment	$400
Online services	$10
Subtotal	*$10,070*
Miscellaneous (roughly 10% of total)	$1,000
Total Expenses	**$11,070**
Projected Income/Expense Total	**$930**

Sample Operating Income/Expenses

Jamie Lynn Hair Designs and Day Spa

Projected Monthly Income	$34,000
Projected Monthly Expenses	
Rent/mortgage	$2,600
Phone	$80
Utilities	$300
Postage	$50
Owner/manager salary	$3,300
Employee wages	$13,417
Benefits/taxes	$3,410
Advertising/promotion	$670
Legal services	
Accounting services	$240
Supplies	$300
Maintenance	$200
Insurance	$50
Magazine subscriptions	$10
Membership dues	$35
Loan repayment	$2,000
Online services	$40
Subtotal	$26,702
Miscellaneous (roughly 10% of total)	$2,670
Total Expenses	**$29,372**
Projected Income/Expense Total	**$4,628**

Operating Income/Expenses Worksheet

Projected Monthly Income	$
Projected Monthly Expenses	
Rent/mortgage	
Phone	
Utilities	
Postage	
Licenses	
Owner/manager salary	
Employee wages	
Benefits/taxes	
Legal services	
Licenses	
Accounting services	
Supplies	
Maintenance	
Insurance	
Magazine subscriptions	
Membership dues	
Loan repayment	
Online services	
Subtotal	
Miscellaneous (roughly 10% of subtotal)	
Total Expenses	$
Projected Income/Expense Total	$

Hair-Raising Truths and Tales

So you've finally plowed your way through the many chapters here outlining the myriad tasks necessary for starting your own salon and spa. You've tackled (and possibly sweated through) the intricacies of financing. You've also considered the requirements of good market research, gnashed your teeth as you reviewed a list of all the taxes you must pay, and bravely faced the reality that you'll need a huge amount of equipment and lots of products to launch this business. For all this effort and commitment, we salute you and hope you will enjoy great success and longevity in your new career.

But even as we wish you the best as you embark on this exciting time of entrepreneurship, we must acknowledge that every new business owner—including you—faces an uphill battle for survival. In fact, the SBA Office of Advocacy says that 56 percent of all new small businesses fail within four years.

Why Businesses Fail

There are many reasons for these failures. Business failure can be due to outside market conditions (such as new competition or unexpected increases in the cost of doing business), financing problems, tax-related issues, poor planning, mismanagement, and a host of other problems.

So what is the problem? The SBA Online Women's Business Center offers these additional common causes of failure:

- *Inadequate cash reserves.* You need at least a six-month cash reserve as a cushion to carry you through until you start making money.
- *Failure to clearly define and understand your market, your customers, and your customers' buying habits.* If you've completed the market analysis discussed in Chapter 3, you know how to address these problems.
- *Failure to price your products or services correctly.* The SBA says you can be the cheapest or the best, but if you try to be both, you'll fail.
- *Failure to anticipate cash flow adequately.* Some suppliers require immediate payment when dealing with new businesses, which can quickly deplete your cash reserves. Add in the months-long wait for reimbursement for anything sold on credit, and you could be seriously cash-strapped.
- *Failure to anticipate or react to competition, technology, or other changes in the marketplace.* When you're busy, it's easy to look the other way while things around you are changing. But just imagine trying to cater to a young, trendy crowd in a community where the population is aging. It won't be long before you find yourself in trouble.
- *Believing you can do everything yourself.* No way. The SBA says one of the biggest challenges entrepreneurs face is being able to loosen their hands on the reins and start delegating to trusted employees. You can't do it all yourself—you must rely on those who have proved they can handle responsibility and make things happen, and then trust their judgment.

Your Plan of Action

So what's a fledgling salon owner to do? To begin with, you should hire professionals like attorneys, accountants, and business managers to assist you in the proper management and operation of your business. Because no matter how enthusiastic, how knowledgeable, and how bright you may be, you're probably not an expert in every field, and your time will only stretch so far. Although in the beginning it can be pretty hard to part with the cash to pay those professional fees, it's worth it in the long run because this kind of help will allow you to focus your attention on the things you do best.

You also should seriously consider learning as much as possible about business management by taking courses at your local community college or university. Knowing at least the basics of finance, accounting, marketing, and the like really can keep you grounded and help you make the right business decisions down the road.

"I really wish I would have understood business better when I started rather than just having industry-specific knowledge," says Dennis Gullo of Moments Salon and Spa in Mount Laurel, New Jersey. "I was an education junkie but only in the salon business. General education focusing on sound business principles is really better because [if you're like me,] no matter how successful you are, your success always feels like luck."

Obviously, the trick is to be such a savvy small-business owner that you don't need luck. Here's a look at some of the resources you have at your disposal that can make you successful.

Words from the Wise

One big benefit you have as a prospective small-business owner is that you can rely on the insight and expertise of the many business owners who have gone before you. Certainly any person who has launched a small business can fill you in on the foibles and follies of entrepreneurship. In addition, other salon and spa owners can be a treasure trove of wisdom. So seriously consider joining one of the industry's many associations, and then network at its conventions or regional meetings. You'll soon learn that even the most successful owners have been where you are and had the same concerns you have today.

> **Tip...**
>
> ### Smart Tip
>
> If you get into a cash-flow crunch, draft a plan to repay your creditors rather than just ignoring them until you have enough money to cover your debts. Most creditors will be willing to work with you because they stand more of a chance of getting their money back if you remain open than if you close.

Even the successful salon and spa owners interviewed for this book recognize that they could have done some things better. For instance, Daryl Jenkins of HairXtreme in Chester, Virginia, says he should have paid more attention to the layout when his wife's salon was designed. "According to conventional business wisdom, you should be earning X number of dollars per square foot, which we weren't doing in the beginning," Jenkins says. "We had a lot of wasted space because everything was so spread out. Of course now it's a good thing, because customers have to go through the styling area to get to the treatment area. That creates good traffic flow that's good for business."

Sasha Rash of La Jolie in Princeton, New Jersey, admits she could have tried to separate herself more from the business in the early days. "As much as I'm a big part of the business, I'm not the whole company," she says. "I was defining myself through the company, and it would have helped if I had accepted the occasional failures more graciously and without so much angst."

Another owner who endured a walk-out and lived to tell the tale says, "I shouldn't have trusted everyone as much as I did. I practically gave them the building, told them not to set it on fire, and then gave them a lighter. Part of the problem was that I wanted to avoid conflict and confrontation and overlooked the need for accountability."

Pat Millar of Millar Salon Spa Store in Clinton, New Jersey, wishes she'd had more money in the beginning to smooth the way. "It's helpful to have a lot of working capital available so you're not leveraging your personal property," Millar says. "But of course when you're younger, you take more risks. And come to think of it, I'm still a risk-taker today."

Stat Fact

The SBA Office of Advocacy characterizes a small business as any independent business with fewer than 500 employees. That means 99.7 percent of all employer firms in the United States are considered to be small businesses, and they employ about half of all private-sector employees.

Debbie Elliot of Debbie Elliott Salon & Day Spa in Portland, Maine, admits she could have been a better manager and leader. "If I had been a leader people could follow, I wouldn't have had to work so many hours and gotten so fried," she confesses. "You can hire good people, but if you don't lead well, they can get funky. Basically, I didn't have control over my own business in the beginning."

Tales from the Trenches

Although every salon/spa owner interviewed for this book could identify something he or she could have done better, in every case these entrepreneurs used creative thinking, hard work, and good old-fashioned determination to meet whatever challenges faced them.

Obviously, this is a strategy that works. They not only survived those scary early years; some of them have been prospering for decades, despite economic uncertainties, personal challenges, and other pressures that have cropped up along the way.

And do they ever have some interesting tales to tell. Neil Ducoff of Salon Business Strategies in Centerbrook, Connecticut, remembers the day when a plump woman who had won a salon services package in a church raffle came into the first salon he ever owned for a hair analysis, perm, and makeup application. Because he was running a lean operation in those days, he was using wrought iron chairs from his parents' backyard for the analysis equipment. The back legs consisted of springy metal strips that allowed the chairs to rock, and when the amply proportioned customer sat down, the chair shot out from under her, flew 20 feet across the salon, and imbedded itself in the sheetrock wall.

"The client fell to the concrete but wasn't hurt," Ducoff says. "She never said a word while we worked and looked very nice when we were finished, but she never returned!"

A Friend Indeed

Sometimes new salon owners end up being mentors themselves despite their relative inexperience in the business, and the rewards are great. Sasha Rash once hired a 30-something woman from a small Caribbean island who came to the United States with $100 in her pocket and little else. She was painfully shy and so limited by her lack of self-confidence that she couldn't make eye contact, even with people she knew.

"From the interview, I could see she had a lot of problems to overcome, but I felt a warmth and drive [from her]," Rash says. "I also knew if I hired her she could make all her dreams come true. And she did. She worked on her self-esteem along with her technical ability, and her life became magical. It took nearly ten years, but she went from a one-room studio rental to owning her own home, a beautiful Mercedes, and a salon of her own."

> **Tip...**
>
> ## Smart Tip
>
> An outside business consultant can help a salon entrepreneur rebound from problems that threaten to destroy his or her business. Sometimes just having a fresh set of eyes look at a problem can result in new solutions that can save the day. If you can find a consultant with salon or spa experience, you'll increase your chances of survival.

Under Construction

Sometimes owners themselves have to overcome great odds to make their own dreams come true. Debbie Elliott had arrived in the Northeast with nothing more than a beat-up car and $4,000 in debts when she heard about a building and an old salon chair that were for sale. When her offer for the building was accepted, she was terrified, especially when she realized it was in such bad shape it should have been condemned. But she doggedly cut and colored hair in that dilapidated shop with tarpaper on the walls and five layers of linoleum on the floor and made repairs when she could. Remarkably, instead of being turned off, her customers were wonderfully supportive, and even looked forward to their appointments so they could see how the renovations were progressing. Today, the small business that started in that ramshackle building is flourishing and has been in *Salon Today*'s top 200 for five consecutive years.

Trying Time

Judy Rice Mangum of Goldwaves in Fort Worth, Texas, had an obstacle of another type to overcome at the start of her business: She had a biopsy and was diagnosed with breast cancer the same day her salon opened. "I had a mastectomy the following Friday and missed the first month Goldwaves was open," Mangum says. "The cancer recurred and I went through chemotherapy and radiation. Not fun. But I worked the whole time and wore a lot of wigs."

She also wore baseball caps with a ponytail sewn inside the back, and eventually patented the idea for the product, which she called Hairhatz. Unfortunately, she had neither the time nor the energy to market it. But happily, her cancer has been in remission for more than a decade.

Urban Legend

Imagine becoming a legend in your own time. That's what has happened to Dennis Gullo of Moments Salon and Spa. Back in 1983, he opened his third salon and decided he shouldn't do hair anymore because he increasingly found himself standing behind the chair and thinking about what he wanted to do with the business instead of teasing hair.

"But I couldn't look my customers in the eye and tell them I didn't do hair anymore," he says. "So I came up with a plan. I went to a surgical supply store, got a fake cast I could wear on my hand, and told everyone that I had torn some ligaments because I was doing karate chops. Eventually the cast came off, and I had to start telling everyone I had nerve damage and had lost my fine motor control. That got their sympathy so they stayed with the salon, and I wasn't stuck behind the chair anymore."

Years later, Gullo was in a Pennsylvania salon talking to the owner about her hair color product line. She happened to mention she had heard a story about a salon owner who was killing himself behind the chair and had started wearing a cast to get out of cutting hair.

"So I'm an urban legend in this industry and lived to hear about it!" Gullo says proudly.

Your Formula for Success

You may never be an urban legend like Gullo, but there's no reason you can't emulate his success—and the success of the many other salon/spa owners featured in this book. If you have drive, determination, and fearless entrepreneurial spirit, everything else will fall into place. Good luck, and long may you (permanently) wave!

Appendix
Hair Salon and
Day Spa Resources

For an industry that offers such specialized services, it's amazing how much information there is in print and in cyberspace about both the hair salon and the day spa industries. The internet is an especially rich source of background information, business tips, and marketing know-how, much of which is posted by people who are themselves in the industry. We've presented some useful resources here, but the list is by no means exhaustive. Also, please note that all contact information was current and accurate at the time of publication.

Associations

Aestheticians International Association Inc.
(469) 429-9300
aiaprofessional.com

American Association of Cosmetology Schools
(800) 831-1086, (480) 281-0431
beautyschools.org

American Electrology Association
electrology.com
infoaea@electrology.com

American Health & Beauty Aids Institute
(708) 633-6328
ahbai.org

▲

American Massage Therapy Association
(877) 905-2700, (847) 864-0123
amtamassage.org
info@amtamassage.org

Black Beauty Supply Association
www.bbsa1.com

Black Owned Beauty Supply Association
(650) 488-4645
bobsaone.org

The Day Spa Association
(201) 865-2065
dayspaassociation.com
info@dayspaassociation.com

International Spa Association
(888) 651-4772, (859) 226-4326
experienceispa.com
ispa@ispastaff.com

National Association of Eco-Friendly Spas and Salons
(877) ECO-VIBE (877-326-8423), ext. 1
naefss.org
tamara@naefss.org

National Certification Board for Therapeutic Massage and Bodywork
(800) 296-0664
ncbtmb.org

National Cosmetology Association
(866) 871-0656
ncacares.org

Professional Beauty Association/The Salon Association
(800) 468-2274, (480) 281-0424
probeauty.org

Professional Beauty Federation
(800) 211-4872

probeautyfederation.org
probeautyfederation@gmail.com

The Salon & Spa Association
salonspaassociation.com

The Spa Association
(866) 291-6231
thespaassociation.com
melinda@spaminton.com

SpaElegance
(877) 200-SPAS
spaelegance.com
info@spaelegance.com

Beauty Institutes

Goldwell Professional Haircare
goldwell-northamerica.com

Paul Mitchell Schools
paulmitchell.com

Blogs

American Salon magazine
americansalonmag.com

American Spa Blog
americanspamag.com

The Beauty Blog Network
beautyblognetwork.com

DAYSPA Beautynista
dayspamagazine.com/blogbeautynista

DSA Spa Industry Blog
dsaprof.wordpress.com

Books

Hairdresser Career Development Systems
(800) 390-4237
hcds4you.com
jon@hcds4you.com

Hairstyling Book Club
American Salon Circulation Inc.
(800) 247-9410
amsaloncir.com
americansaloncir@worldnet.att.net

Chat Rooms and Message Boards

Beauty Tech
beautytech.com/livechat

Salon Channel
salonchannel.com

Continuing Education

Bob Jones University
(800) 252-6363
bju.edu

Delta College
(989) 686-9000
delta.edu

Golden State University
goldenstateuniversity.edu
info@goldenstateuniversity.com

Hairdresser Career Development Systems
(800) 390-4237
hcds4you.com
jon@hcds4you.com

Montcalm Community College
(877) 328-2111, (989) 328-2111
montcalm.edu

Santa Monica College
(310) 434-4592
smc.edu

Skyline College
(650) 738-4100
skylinecollege.net

Gift Card Program Providers

Merchant Consulting Group
(978) 744-9090
merchantconsultinggroup.com

PlasticGiftCardsOnline.com
(800) 808-7472
plasticgiftcardsonline.com

SmartCardSupply.com
(800) 331-3921
smartcardsupply.com

Valuetec
(888) 381-8258
valuetec.net

Zebra Card Printer Solutions
(800) 452-4056, (805) 579-1800
zebracard.com

Hair-Care Franchises

BoRics
Regis Corp.
(952) 947-7777
regiscorp.com

▲

Cartoon Cuts
(800) 701-CUTS (2887),
954-653-CUTS (2887)
cartooncuts.com
info@cartooncuts.com

Cost Cutters Family Hair Salon
Regis Corp.
costcutters.com

Fantastic Sams Hair Salons
fantasticsams.com

Fun Cuts 4 Kids and Adults
(901) 752-4FUN (4386)
funcuts4kids.com

Great Clips Inc.
(800) 473-2825
greatclips.com

Lemon Tree Family Hair Salons
(516) 393-5860
lemontree.com

Master Cuts
Regis Corp.
(952) 947-7777
mastercuts.com

Pro-Cuts Franchise Corp.
procuts.com

Regis Corp.
(952) 947-7777
regiscorp.com

Snip N' Clip
(800) 622-6804, (913) 345-0077
snipnclip.net
info@snipnclip.net

Sport Clips
(888) 952-2130
sportclips.com
info@sportclips.com

Supercuts
Regis Corp.
supercuts.com

The Yellow Balloon
(818) 760-7141
theyellowballoon.com
info@theyellowballoon.com

Marketing Services

Day Spa Marketing LLC
dayspamarketing.com
info@dayspamarketing.com

Merchant Accounts

Capital Merchant Solutions Inc.
(877) 495-2419
takecardstoday.com

Credit Card Processing Services
(888) 717-1245
ccps.biz
Kevin@ccps.biz

InfoMerchant
(971) 223-5632
infomerchant.net

Merchant Accounts Express
(888) 845-9457
merchantexpress.com

Total Merchant Services
(888) 871-4558
merchant-account-4U.com
info@21cr.com

Merchant Account Alternative

PayPal
PayPal.com

Professional Salon Product Manufacturers

Aveda Corp.
(800) 644-4831
aveda.com

Bioelements
(800) 433-6650
bioelements.com

Bumble and bumble
(866) 513-0498
bumbleandbumble.com

Clairol Professional
(800) 221-4900
clairolpro.com

Goldwell Professional Haircare
goldwell-northamerica.com

Matrix
L'Oreal USA
(888) 777-6396
matrix.com

Nioxin
(800) 628-9890, (770) 944-1308
nioxin.com

Paul Mitchell Systems & Hair Products
paulmitchell.com

Revlon
(800) 473-8566
revlon.com

Rusk
(800) USE-RUSK
rusk1.com

Sebastian International Inc.
(800) 347-4424
sebastian-intl.com

Tigi Hair Care
(800) 259-8596
tigihaircare.com
customerservice@tigihaircare.com

Wella Professionals
(800) 935-5273
wellausa.com

Professional Salon/Spa Supplies and Equipment

Aveda Institute
(800) 644-4831
avedapurepro.com

Belvedere Co.
(800) 435-5491, (815) 544-3131
Canada (800) 463-0229
belvedereco.com

CacheBeauty.com
(800) 643-0333
cachebeauty.com
customerservice@cachebeauty.com

Cameo Beauty
(800) 645-9542, (631) 598-1130
cameobeauty.com

Custom Craftworks
(800) 627-2387
customcraftworks.com
info@customcraftworks.com

Folicapro.com
(888) 919-4247
folicapro.com

Salon Equipment International
(877) 461-2972
salonequipmentintl.com

SalonFurniture.com
(800) 345-2924 (eastern U.S.);
(888) 345-2945 (western U.S.)
salonfurniture.com

Spa Equipment International
(877) 461-2972
spaequipmentintl.com

Takara Belmont
(732) 469-5000
takara-belmont.com

SpaEquip Inc.
(877) 778-1682
spaequip.com
assist@spaequip.com

Publications

American Salon
Questex Media Group
americansalonmag.com

American Spa
Questex Media Services
americanspamag.com

DAYSPA **Magazine**
Creative Age
(800) 442-5667, (818) 782-7328
dayspamag.com

Hair News **Magazine**
hair-news.com

Interhair

interhair.com

Massage **Magazine**
Massage Mag Inc.
(888) 883-3801
massagemag.com
cstsrv@massagemag.com

Modern Salon
Vance Publishing Corp.
(800) 808-2623, (847) 634-2600
modernsalon.com

NAILS **Magazine**
Bobit Publishing Co.
(310) 533-2400
nailsmag.com

Salon Today
Vance Publishing Corp.
(847) 634-2600
salontoday.com
info@vancepublishing.com

Salon/Day Spa Owners

Andrew Marké Salon
Angela Marke
(586) 948-8200
andrewmarkesalon.com

Goldwaves Salon & Spa
Judy Rice Mangum and Leslie Rice
(817) 731-8888
goldwavessalon.com

Hair One
Dennis Gullo
(856) 234-8875
hairone.com
information@hairone.com

HairXtreme
Daryl Jenkins

(804) 748-2090
HairXtreme.com
info@HairXtreme.com

La Jolie Salon
Sasha Rash
(609) 924-1188
lajoliesalon.com

Lorinda's Salon Spa & Store
Lorinda Warner
(425) 743-9722
lorindassalon.com
manager@lorindassalon.com

Millar Salon Spa Store
Pat Millar
(908) 735-5170

Scizzors
John Palmieri
scizzors.com
john@scizzors.com

Salon/Day Spa Software

Leprechaun Spa and Salon Software
(800) 373-1684
leprechaun-software.com
sales@leprechaun-software.com

Millennium
Harms Software Inc.
(888) 813-2141
harms-software.com
sales@harms-software.com

QuickPlan Salon
(800) 417-7017
quickplan.com

Salon Iris Software
CMJ Designs Inc.
(888) 803-4747

saloniris.com
sales@cmjdesigns.com

Unique Salon Software
Unique Salon Software Inc.
(800) 586-4783, (817) 459-1147
salonpages.com
uniquesalonsoftware@gmail.com

Salon Management Resources

Hairdresser Career Development Systems
(800) 390-4237
hcds4you.com
jon@hcds4you.com

Salon Business Strategies
Strategies Publishing Group Inc.
(800) 417-4848
strategiespub.com

Trade Shows

America's Beauty Show
(800) 883-7808, (312) 494-3040
americasbeautyshow.com

Cosmoprof North America
cosmoprofnorthamerica.com

Global Hair & Beauty Expo
(209) 824-0041
ghbexpo.com

INsalon
(888) 213-0949, (952) 925-9731
sspatoday.com

International Beauty Show New York
International Beauty Group

(800) 427-2420
ibsnewyork.com

**International Esthetics, Cosmetics &
Spa Conferences**
Questex Media Group
iecsc.com

International Hair and Nail Show
(800) 676-SHOW
ihshow.com
info@ihshow.com

International Salon & Spa Exposition
probeauty.org

Web Hosting/Domain Names

DOMAIN.com
domain.com

EarthLink
earthlink.net

GoDaddy.com
godaddy.com

HostMonster
hostmonster.com

IPOWERWEB
ipowerweb.com

SBC Webhosting.com
webhosting.com

Yahoo!
yahoo.com

Website Development

Day Spa Marketing LLC
dayspamarketing.com
info@dayspamarketing.com

Elbel Consulting Services LLC
elbelconsultingservices.com

Website, Miscellaneous

Dreadlocks.com
dreadlocks.com

HairOnLine.com
hairol.com

Glossary

Accupressure: a holistic healing technique that uses the fingers to press on certain points of the body to relieve pain and stress and promote healing.

Aesthetician (or esthetician): a person who specializes in the business of beauty and is usually licensed by the state in which he/she does business.

Aromatherapy: the use of aromatic botanical extracts to balance and promote the health of the body, mind, and spirit.

Autoclave: a piece of equipment used to sterilize personal care implements. In a salon/spa, the autoclave is used for scissors, and manicure and pedicure tools.

Back bar: a cabinet (usually above the shampoo bowl) that holds products used on clients' hair, including shampoo and conditioner. Back-bar inventory is tracked as part of a salon's cost of doing business. The back bar may be part of a backwash unit that includes a shampoo bowl and a chair.

Backgrounder: a news release that gives general information about your business that will spur the local media to do a more in-depth story about your company and services.

▲

Balenotherapy: a type of hydrotherapy that uses fresh water (vs. sea water).

Blog: short for "web log;" a personal online journal that's updated frequently and read widely.

Body mask: botanical compounds (including mud, paraffin, seaweed, and herbs) used to moisturize and tone the skin while stimulating circulation.

Body wrap: wrappings made of linen, rubber, plastic, foil, or other materials that are wrapped snuggly (but not to the point of constriction) to seal in body masks or other substances during treatment. The wraps promote product absorption, heat, and detoxification, and are used to temporarily diminish the appearance of cellulite.

Booth rental: renting space to a cosmetologist (hair stylist, manicurist, etc.) who is not employed directly by the salon. The owner is considered the landlord, and the booth renter is an independent contractor who's responsible for paying his or her own taxes, providing his or her own tools, etc.

Chakras: the seven centers of spiritual energy in the human body, according to yoga philosophy; the chakras run the length of the spine and include the root, sex, stomach, heart, throat, brow, and crown.

Contingency fee: payment for legal services taken as a percentage of a settlement (often 25 percent or higher).

Cosmetologist: an expert in the use of equipment and products used in the beauty business; cosmetologists may be trained in procedures like hair cutting and styling, hair coloring, manicuring, facial treatments, makeup, and electrolysis, as well as beauty salon management.

dba: acronym for "doing business as"; refers to the legal name under which you are operating.

Deep-tissue massage: a type of massage that manipulates deep tissues of the body to stimulate recirculation and regenerate lymphatic flow. Despite the name "deep," pressure is not necessary for this type of massage.

Depilation: hair removal; includes electrolysis (permanent hair removal technique); and waxing and threading (temporary hair removal techniques).

Demographics: socioeconomic characteristics of a selected population, including age, gender, income, occupation, income, and so on.

Electrologist: a hair removal specialist.

Electrolysis: a painless process that uses a low electric current or laser to destroy unwanted hair follicles, thus removing them permanently.

Enzyme peel: a type of exfoliating skin treatment, usually applied like a mask, which uses natural substances to dissolve dead skin.

Essential oils: highly concentrated aromatic extracts used for aromatherapy and massage.

Exfoliation: the process of removing, peeling, or sloughing off dead or dry skin cells from the body, using salts, polishes, and other means, including mechanical.

Facebook: a multimedia social networking website with profiles, photos, and videos created by the "owner," and a "wall" where friends and visitors can post messages. Differs from MySpace because it's possible to add "apps," or small programs, that expand Facebook's capabilities.

Facial chair: a specialized reclining chair that's raised and lowered by means of a hydraulic foot pump to make it easier for the aesthetician to service a client while providing skin-care treatments.

Healing stones: gemstones or crystals in rough or polished form used on the chakras and other parts of the body to heal, soothe, and protect. Some types of healing stones include adventurine, carnelian, emerald, jade, moonstone, and ruby.

Hot stone massage: a type of therapeutic massage that uses warmed stones to transmit healing energy; gemstones may also be used for the same purpose.

Hydrotherapy: the use of water to maintain and restore health.

Hydrotherapy tub: device used to deliver a type of underwater massage that relieves stress and muscle spasms.

LinkedIn: a business-oriented social networking site used for professional networking.

Mail merge: the process of merging an address file with a letter file to create personalized letters, usually for a mass mailing.

Manual lymph drainage: an advanced type of massage that uses rhythmic, light strokes to stimulate the lymphatic system; said to remove congestion and reduce swelling by helping the flow of lymph toward the heart.

Media kit: a packet that contains publicity and sales materials about a company and its services.

Meta tag: a special HTML (computer language) tag used to store information about a website but which isn't displayed on the site itself; used by search engines to index websites.

MySpace: a social networking website consisting of personal information, photos, blogs, and other information of interest to the person who posts it.

▲

Napptural hair: African American hair that hasn't been altered by chemical processes like hair relaxers, jherri curls, silkeners, and texturizers.

Psychographics: the attitudes of your target audience, which are useful for determining why a consumer uses your services or products.

Reflexology: a holistic therapy that stimulates the feet, hands, and ears to encourage natural healing, reduce stress, eliminate toxins, and revitalize the body.

Reiki: a Japanese technique of relaxation and stress reduction that promotes healing; the word translates to universal ("rei") energy ("ki").

Rollabout: a cart with drawers used in the salon to store hair stylists' equipment; sometimes used in place of a regular stylist's station.

Salt glow: a therapeutic mixture of sea salt (often from the Dead Sea), minerals and/or other botanical extracts, and essential oils that are massaged onto the skin to scrub off dead skin cells, and polish and buff the skin.

Shiatsu massage: a type of massage in which certain acupressure points are manipulated to heal and improve circulation.

Swedish massage: the most popular type of massage in the United States and Canada, which uses the hands, forearms, or elbows to manipulate muscles as a way of improving mental and physical health and decreasing stress.

Swiss shower: a type of water massage that sprays water at specific areas of the body to stimulate circulation; also used to remove body masks like salt glows and to provide post-treatment relaxation.

Teaser: a clever or evocative line of copy, often on the outside of an envelope, that entices the reader to read further.

Thalassotherapy: a type of hydrotherapy that uses sea water as a therapeutic treatment.

Threading: temporary hair removal technique that uses sewing thread twisted in a continuous motion to remove hair

Twitter: a social networking service in which users send short (140 character) messages (or "microblogs") to a select group of "followers"; the messages are called "tweets."

Vichy shower: an apparatus that rains either warm or cold water from above the client and is used to rinse off body masks.

Viral marketing: marketing that encourages people to pass along a marketing message; typically viral marketing facilitators include blogs, LinkedIn, and Twitter.

Walk-out: A situation in which salon staff—usually the stylists—quit simultaneously so they can start their own salon. This situation is fairly common in the salon industry—common enough to warrant this note in the Glossary.

Wet room: a spa treatment room with "wet" services, including Vichy shower or hydrotherapy.

Index